AFRICA

An Artist's Journal

KIM DONALDSON

A F R

I C A

An Artist's Journal

K I M   D O N A L D S O N

PAVILION

Vervet monkey

FOREWORD

Whilst this journal is certainly a testimony to Kim Donaldson's commitment to the flora and fauna of Africa, what clearly distinguishes this book of wildlife art from others on the same subject are the particular qualities of the artist himself.

I first saw Kim Donaldson's work in an exhibition at a London gallery – incidentally, this is where my passion for collecting started – and in 1994 I purchased my first Kim Donaldson: a pastel of a black rhino. In my opinion, Kim is one of those very rare wildlife artists who is not only able to capture the physical look of the animal he is portraying, but also its spirit. He is able to depict the animal in all its dignity, caught in a specific moment, creating an almost tangible presence on the canvas.

Kim Donaldson is a man who is in all senses the 'real thing': a bushman and an exceptional artist who combines these skills to create an authentic taste of Africa.

Travelling alone, sometimes spending weeks in the bush, Kim has traversed the differing terrain of the many countries that make up the vast African continent in search of particular places in order to capture on canvas what has become his lifelong passion – wildlife in all its guises.

I believe Kim's art makes you a participant in his personal safari. We can only marvel at the insights he brings to his work: vast horizons clouded by mirages on which huge herds of Cape buffalo appear to float; the intimate restful moments of the big cats; the poise of the antelope; and the gigantic grace of the elephant.

During his sojourns, Kim has witnessed the shifting changes in attitude to conservation and the varying attempts, both good and misguided, that affect the wildlife he loves.

That he cares about the animals he records is so evidently clear in the images he produces, and his art reflects his respect for their right to remain unfettered. As he says, 'Awareness, education, management and money are four fundamental ingredients in the recipe required for successful conservation. If our generation is serious about "leaving something behind", we need to get involved and support organizations that can represent us.'

We could all learn so much from artists like Kim who are showing us the awesome beauty and incredible sights of the natural world. Hopefully, we will learn that it must be saved at all costs from the exploitation of the past – which unfortunately often continues today – if we are to preserve and to co-exist with our natural heritage.

I feel honoured to share and experience the very special and personal places that Kim has spent a lifetime observing.

The talent and vision of this acclaimed artist are here for all to see, and long may he continue to provide us with such wonderful images.

Lord Robin Russell, June 2001

ACKNOWLEDGEMENTS

Even in a solo book of paintings, there are so many people who play a role and help both directly and indirectly. I have had the support of my family and friends. Their encouragement has been with me for many years culminating in the production of this book.

My mother, Aletta, deserves special mention for my early days as does my ever-supportive wife, Lydia, who has played a major role over the past 25 years.

I would like to use this opportunity to thank my artist friends whose talents have pushed me so hard to compete. They are individually acknowledged in the Roll of Honour (p. 213).

My cousin, Stretch Ferreira of Goliath Safaris, who has gone beyond the call of duty, I thank. Likewise, thanks go to my friends Dr Harold and Jeanne Bloch and Ben and Engela Marais for their generous support.

To the directors of Washington Green Ltd I express my heartful thanks and appreciation for allowing me the artistic freedom to make my own mistakes. Sally Antrobus deserves much more than the title of editor for making my text readable. Her patience, understanding and comprehension not only of Africa but of a confused artist's attempt to project his own story in his own way has been invaluable.

To all my collectors who have contributed by their interest in my work, my thanks.

To my brother-in-law, Patrick Manders, who set my computer up and answered my cries of frustration without complaint, I owe a great deal.

The most important person in this whole endeavour has been left for last – Lester Allison is not only a true friend but a man who stepped up to the plate. Without question, he saw my need for this book, wanted to be part of it and made it happen.

This book is dedicated to
Lester Allison III.
An extraordinary friend.

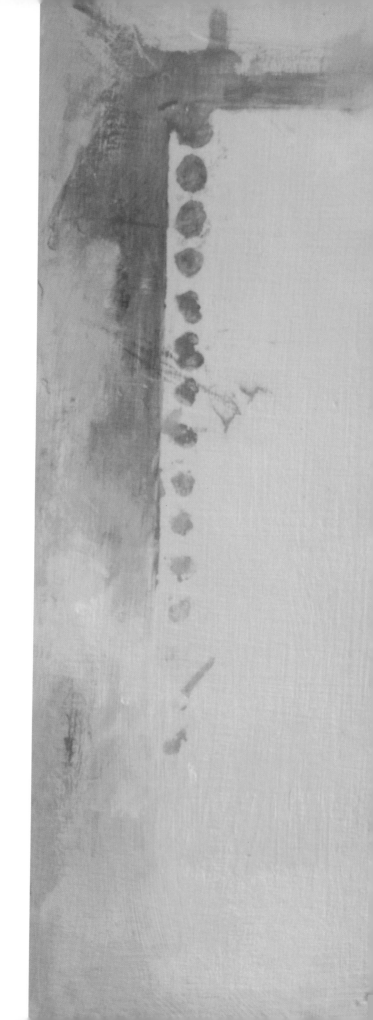

First published in Great Britain in 2001 by
PAVILION BOOKS LIMITED
London House, Great Eastern Wharf,
Parkgate Road, London SW11 4NQ
www.pavilionbooks.co.uk

Text and illustrations © Kim Donaldson 2001
Design and layout © Pavilion Books Limited 2001

The moral right of the author and illustrator has been asserted

Designed by Guy Callaby for Washington Green Etcetera

A CIP catalogue record for this book is available from the British Library.

ISBN 1 86205 482 7

Printed in Italy by Giunti Industrie Grafiche

2 4 6 8 10 9 7 5 3

This book can be ordered direct from the publisher.
Please contact the Marketing Department. But try your bookshop first.

CONTENTS

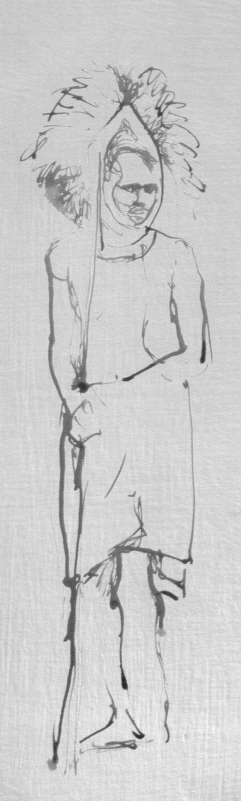

Opposite: Abstract elephant

INTRODUCTION

Some months after beginning this book, I began to question the wisdom of it all. Several people who were invaluable to the project trusted me without question and the responsibility bore down on me like a ton of bricks. Who was I to attempt such an undertaking? I could see my old English teacher from my school days falling off his chair with uncontrollable laughter after hearing that his worst student was writing a book. The self-doubt lingered for a long time until one day, a friend of mine asked, 'Why would you want to do a book anyway?' The question played on my mind. But then things suddenly sharpened into focus and in a flash I was released from my anxiety – I was doing this because I love art, books and Africa. It was justified

in my mind – this was my qualification. Suddenly, being a gifted writer or an experienced scientist were not the necessary requirements. I apologize just once for any errors in the text or my journals. I do however ask something of you: do not view this book with a critical mind, looking to analyse and find deep meaning. Look at this for what it is – a collection of work that represents a wonderful period of travel in a unique continent. Look at this as a personal invitation to share my safaris and art.

Africa has seen dramatic changes in recent decades. At times it is difficult to be positive about its future but as I am not politically motivated, I've tried to stay away from these issues and remain upbeat. The only real issues addressed

involve conservation, and even these I have approached with conscious restraint. This is, after all, a celebration, and I don't want anyone spoiling my party.

It is difficult to produce *one* volume on Africa. There are so many wilderness areas and animal and bird species worthy of inclusion. The history of the continent and amazing array of characters who played a part, even if one were considering only the notable wildlife areas, would add up to many volumes. Much of the work I originally planned fell by the wayside. There are therefore many places, interesting people and wildlife species that have been excluded. The criteria I placed upon myself were that I would only include areas I have travelled

things. He converses with people of different races and benefits from their combined knowledge; his comprehension is exceptional although derived from life and listening rather than from the printed word. But the most important thing I have learnt from this man and others with whom I have shared a bush campfire with is the importance of *silence*.

There is a silence in those who don't need to boast and I am very respectful of the silent ones, for when they speak they have much to convey.

MOST VISITORS first experience Africa through the windows of a zebra-striped minivan, being introduced to the animals, the savanna and the Rift Valley. The mild discomforts of dust, bumpy roads and biting flies are short-lived – dispelled when one is refreshed and rejuvenated each evening at a lodge catering to one's every need. After such a

trip, many people feel drawn in by the magic of Africa and have stories to tell and experiences to take home.

It is, however, only when you challenge the senses and walk where the animals walk that Africa fully touches you. We have to leave the comforts and security of our other world behind; we need to place ourselves in a situation where our senses become survival equipment. This is when we can engage with Africa. Back home, when you hear someone telling a story about how a buffalo charged the minivan or about a close call with an angry elephant, you will be able to allow yourself a quiet smile, for you know it is possible to talk the talk without having walked the walk.

I invite you to share my explorations of Africa through my journals, art and travels. I hope this record will encourage you to walk the walk and come to know the silence.

personally, and that this collection of work would evolve and not be contrived. I have visited some of the places covered many times and some of them only very briefly. But I know the value of the African proverb: 'He who does not travel does not know the value of men'. I learnt a long time ago to keep my mouth shut and to listen to what others have to say. I have been privileged to have met some of Africa's special people, men and women who have lived the hard, simple lives of frontier people. Through them I came to appreciate both the delights and the demands the country has to offer. I have learnt about the ways of the bushveld, its people and wildlife. One extraordinary character and good friend, Bill McGill, can not only name all manner of things, in English, Afrikaans, Zulu and Tswana, but also knows how they interact and relate to one another in the larger scheme of

A day's bag is arranged for a photograph while the hounds get a well-deserved rest. Courtesy of the National Archives of Zimbabwe

Lions of the Serengeti

AS A STUDENT, I found history to be of little interest. I couldn't get excited about the Battle of Hastings or the French Revolution when I lived in the spacious African upland then called Southern Rhodesia. Endless years spent learning names and dates, parrot fashion, of places and events in faraway lands fortunately came to an end when our curriculum switched to African history. Suddenly history became of

THE EARLY DAYS

value and I studied it with a renewed interest. David Livingstone, John Speke and Richard Burton were heroic men who paved the way for a host of hunters, explorers, botanists and artists. As these adventurers journalized, mapped, illustrated and published their experiences, so grew the mystique of Africa, and as the word spread, the great African safari began. It is somewhat surprising to realize that this period lasted less than a hundred years.

Africa 1791 D'anville, courtesy of the National Archives of Zimbabwe

The quagga once roamed southern Africa in substantial numbers. It was one of the first animals in Africa to become extinct following the arrival of European settlers.

equus quagga quagga (extinct)   KimDonaldson

'Nothing is wanting, nothing is superfluous, the smallest weed or insect is indispensably necessary to the general good. Nothing more bespeaks a littleness of mind, than to regard as useless all that does not visibly benefit man.'

William Burchell

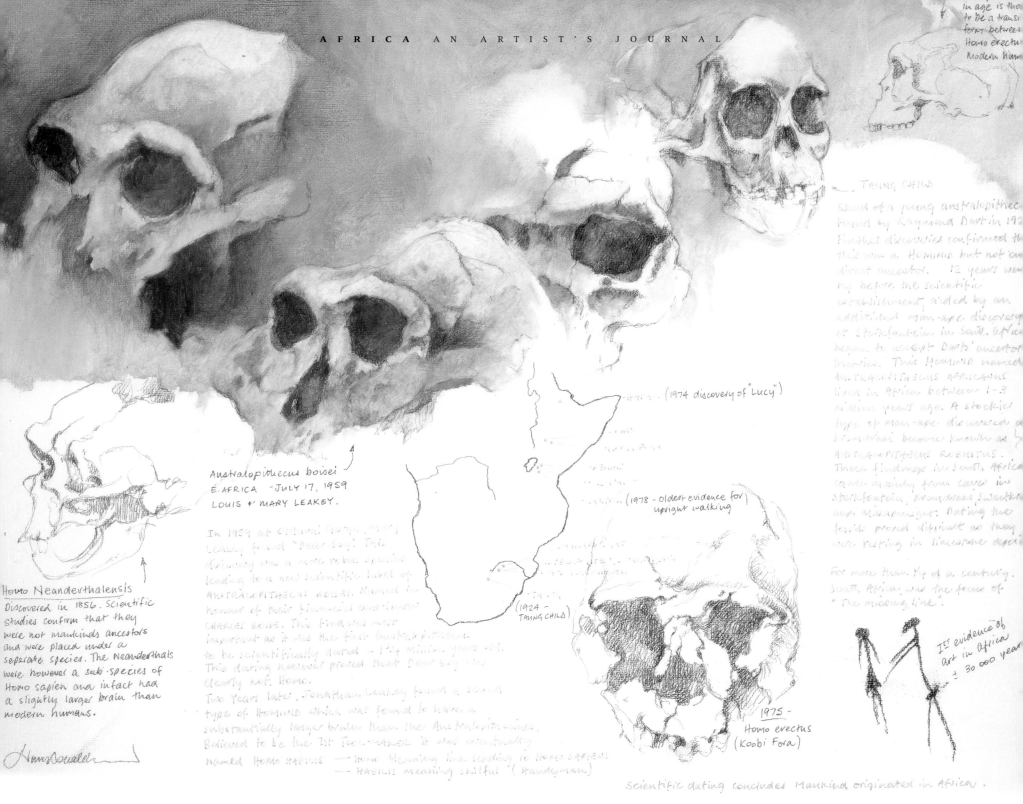

Homo Neanderthalensis
Discovered in 1856. Scientific
studies confirm that they
were not mankinds ancestors
and were placed under a
seperate species. The Neanderthals
were however a sub-species of
Homo sapien and infact had
a slightly larger brain than
modern humans.

Australopithecus boisei
E. AFRICA - JULY 17, 1959
LOUIS & MARY LEAKEY.

In 1959 at Olduvai Gorge, Mary
Leakey found "Dear Boy". This
discovery was a more robus species
leading to a new scientific level of
AUSTRALOPITHECUS BOISEI. Named in
honour of their financial contributor
CHARLES BOISE. This find was most
important as it was the first Australopithecus
to be scientifically dated — 1¾ million years old.
This dating however proved that Dear boy was
clearly not Homo.
Two Years later, Jonathan Leakey found a second
type of HOMINID which was found to have a
substantially larger brain than the Australopithecines.
Believed to be the 1st TOOL-MAKER it was eventually
named HOMO HABILIS — Homo Meaning line leading to Homo SAPIENS
— HABILIS meaning skilful (Handyman)

(1974 discovery of "LUCY")

(1978 - oldest evidence for)
upright walking

(1924 -
TAUNG CHILD)

1975 -
Homo erectus
(Koobi Fora)

1st evidence of
Art in Africa
± 30 000 years

Scientific dating concludes Mankind originated in Africa.

TAUNG CHILD
Skull of a young australopithecus
found by Raymond Dart in 1924.
Further discoveries confirmed that
this was a HOMINID but not our
direct ancestor. 12 years went
by before the scientific
establishment, aided by an
additional man-ape discovery
at Sterkfontein in South Africa
began to accept Dart's ancestor
theories. This HOMINID named
AUSTRALOPITHECUS AFRICANUS
lived in Africa between 1-3
million years ago. A stockier
type of man-ape discovered at
Kromdraai became known as
AUSTRALOPITHECUS ROBUSTUS.
These findings in South Africa
came mainly from caves in
Sterkfontein, Kromdraai, Swartkrans
and Makapansgat. Dating these
fossils proved difficult as they
were resting in limestone deposits.

For more than ½ a century,
South Africa was the focus of
"The missing link".

*Origins of
mankind*

Broken Hill Man (second from the left)
was found in 1921 on Kabwe (Broken
Hill), Zambia. He was somewhere
between late Homo erectus and early
Homo sapiens and probably lived
about 100,000 years ago. Courtesy of
the National Archives of Zimbabwe.

Even though the Cape – the southernmost tip of Africa – was occupied by the Europeans as of the 1600s, the interior remained *terra incognita* for the settlers and inland travel was discouraged by the early Dutch administration. In 1806 Britain was at war with Holland and took control of the Cape, inheriting the Dutch policy of discouraging travel to the north. In 1811 a remarkable young botanist named William Burchell left the Cape on a four-year expedition. Although his primary interest lay in collecting botanical specimens, his natural enthusiasm to learn about this new world and its native peoples earned him a permanent place in history. His expedition resulted in volumes of journals in which he meticulously recorded and illustrated everything he encountered. Burchell collected 40,000 botanical specimens, made hundreds of drawings and was responsible for charting the finest map of southern Africa.

When Burchell's engravings and journals were published in 1822, they enthralled another remarkable young adventurer named William Cornwallis Harris and fuelled his hunting and his artistic imagination. Harris arrived in the Cape in 1836, a full generation before the likes of Livingstone, Burton and Speke set foot in Africa, but already the land was changing. The Cape Colony had been heavily hunted and several species of animals indigenous to the area were no longer found there. Harris did arrive in time to encounter and record the great

migration of the springbok, known as the trekbokken by the Dutch. The number of these tiny gazelles was so enormous that as they moved through the area, the countryside was stripped bare and animals at the rear died of starvation. That same year was also the beginning of a considerable human exodus. Between 1836 and 1838, several thousand Afrikaners left the Cape and British rule and made their way northwards, settling in what became known as the Orange Free State and the Transvaal.

A cross between a zebra and a donkey looks remarkably like the extinct quagga.

Cornwallis Harris's manner of recording the animals in their natural setting is evident today in their anatomical accuracy – accuracy that was seriously lacking in the work of artists who used museum specimens and mounted trophies as models. Harris succeeded where the Afrikaners failed and obtained the permission of the Matabele king, Mzilikazi, to hunt and travel in his territory. This was big game country, alive with elephant, lion, buffalo, rhinoceros and hippopotamus and he was finally

able to experience Burchell's Africa.

Like Cornwallis Harris, another character was drawn to Africa but unlike Harris, he did not have an artist's appreciation for the beauty of the wild creatures. He came only to hunt and kill. His name was Roualeyn Gordon-Cumming, a self-styled individual who would have made his presence known on any continent in any era. Livingstone said he hunted like 'a mad sort of Scotsman', and Gordon-Cumming's own writings indeed reveal him to be kindred to those who fought to the death at the Battle of Culloden. Gordon-Cumming did not stay and build a home in Africa but rather took what he wanted and then left. He did, however, take back to the rest of the world his commanding presence, his stories of Africa, and 30 tons of Africana to exhibit in a travelling display.

Overlapping Gordon-Cumming's stay in Africa was the visit of a young adventurer who epitomized everything proper. William Cotton Oswell travelled the country with a sense of decency and fairness, leaving a lasting impression on those who met him. He was described by Sir Samuel Baker, a man not easily impressed, as 'full of fearlessness and kindness, six feet, sinewy and muscular, with an eagle glance, a first rate horseman, powerful, enduring, the perfection of a Nimrod, without a rival and without an enemy, the greatest hunter ever known in modern times, the truest friend and most thorough example of an English gentleman' (in Bull 1988: 65-67).

I started my career in the newspaper industry and will always be a 'newspaper man'. The early newspapers were written by hand and a delight to read. Today they give us a valuable insight as this 1892 copy shows; although it was published only a couple of years after the Pioneer Column of 1890, there was already a doctor, dentist, lawyer and building contractor in town offering their services.

Milk delivery in Gwelo township, southern Rhodesia, circa 1906

All photographs and historic references on these two pages are courtesy of the National Archives of Zimbabwe.

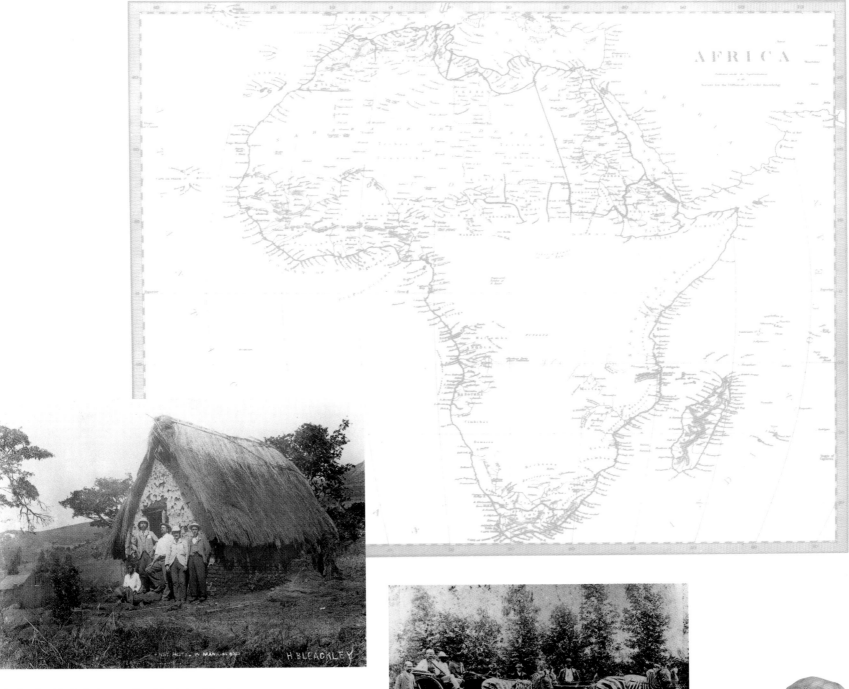

The first hotel in Penhalonga valley, Manicaland Province,
southern Rhodesia, circa 1896

Attempts at using zebra in the role of the horse,
mule or donkey failed. Date unknown.

Oswell played a hand in Africa by setting the standard. He was troubled by the future, concerned for the game and the people, and he showed compassion and understanding far in advance of all other foreigners. Thomas Baines, artist and explorer, and the hunters William Charles Baldwin, Arthur Neumann and Frederick C. Selous recorded their experiences. Selous made Africa his home and died on its soil after a long adventurous life. These early writings were a compendium of adventure that drew more travellers to African shores. Some of them were interested in much more than just the hunting. The scramble for Africa had begun, and along with it came the more powerful and the most dangerous of men – politicians. European countries took it upon themselves to divide up and colonize the African continent. For the most part, their ventures under the umbrella of 'civilizing' took advantage of the local inhabitants and raped the terrain of its natural wealth. There is a case to be made that this had many positive benefits to Africa, as the Europeans brought modern medicine, religion and literacy, and developed these backward regions, but there was also pillage and the results are with us yet.

Wildlife did benefit from some of these endeavours. It is interesting to note, for example, that the great wildebeest migration of the Serengeti did not previously exist in today's magnitude. Rinderpest and other natural conditions kept the animal populations down. The human population also grew with the help of modern medicine, and the wilderness became threatened by the demands of the people. Wherever there are too many people, controls and rules need to be implemented. The first order of business was to protect the land and the animals. This was achieved by demarcating areas as reserves. South Africa's Kruger National Park became a shining example and the standard for several other countries to follow. Large but artificially bounded areas, mostly controlled by government, are absolutely necessary to the future of the fauna and flora of Africa, the only way to protect it for coming generations.

Although Africans and Europeans may differ in their attitudes to wild animals and land use, it has become abundantly clear to all that it makes good economic sense to conserve wild places. Much has changed in a very short span of time. Dramatic changes will continue to take place. I am grateful for my exposure to wild Africa and for being a witness to its entry into the modern world. Africa has much to teach us, in many dimensions, but if there is one thing that I have learnt it is that it will never be tamed.

I personally wouldn't want it any other way.

During a four year expediti[on] the english botanist W. J. collecting 40,000 botani[cal] several new species of a having the zebra specie[s] him. (commonly known as

the Cape (commencing in 1811)
nell was credited with
ecimens and discovering
5. He is honoured by
uus burchelli named after
Burchell's zebra.)

Burchell's zebra

Lion portraiture

SOUTH

Cape Point

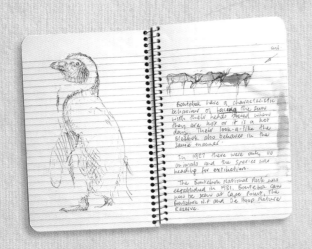

SOUTH AFRICA IS ONE of the largest, most varied countries in Africa, much of it south of the tropics. The seas along the Cape became notorious as they battered and wrecked many ships and survivors often became residents. This was the case with my great-grandfather, a Portuguese sailor. After being shipwrecked off the Cape of Good Hope, he ended up staying in South Africa. At the time, the Cape was under British rule so he was directed to the French district which was occupied by the Huguenots. There he met and married a French girl, settled in the Eastern Cape and became one of the founding citizens of a new society. South Africa is a composite of people from different worlds and a new language and culture were born.

AFRICA

These early immigrants, through ignorance and possibly greed, were responsible for killing wild animals on a grand scale which led to the extinction of several species. Their descendants however, in a kind of reparation, are responsible for introducing the most advanced conservation programmes in Africa. Land was and continues to be set aside in an effort to protect it in its natural state. It is part of the heritage that South Africans hold dear. Their love for the bushveld and their country borders on arrogance. The road signs used in Texas to deter littering: 'Don't mess with Texas', are akin to the way a South African would address a similar situation.

*C*ultural and racial differences have been well chronicled and the saga continues. I lived in South Africa for 14 years and I believe that for all its faults, South Africa got a bad rap in the press. It is a truly wonderful country and my adopted home. One hopes that South Africans will come to grips with their difficult problems to the benefit of all the people, wildlife and diverse environments.

The years I spent in South Africa were the happiest of my life. They included the beginning of my career as an artist and my choice to specialize in wildlife art gave me the opportunity to travel and experience the bush like few others. I travelled to the far corners of southern Africa in my quest to get reference material and to arm myself with the necessary knowledge to paint my subject well. It was a labour of love that moulded me into the person I am today. Always happy with my own company, I mainly travelled solo and I would go days without seeing or talking to another person. Over the years I developed a preference for travelling this way and camping out in the bush by myself whenever I could.

As Cape Town was my first city of residence in South Africa, the first place I visited was the Cape coast. So different from the bushveld of what was then Rhodesia, where I had spent my childhood. I was very taken with this land of the fynbos. Mountain ranges reared almost vertically on either side of the Cape flats. The volatile weather and strong winds threw the surf against the rugged coastline. The rocks, coloured in orange and an array of greys by lichen, contrasted with the muted green of the foliage. The plants are sculptured by the continuous winds, and the stunted trees, bent and twisted by these winds, look crippled and tortured.

There are several proclaimed parks in the Cape that play an important role in protecting the fynbos and plant and animal species that are indigenous to the area. This is the home of the bontebok, the Cape mountain zebra, gnu and extinct blue buck, all of which had their very existence threatened to some degree by the early settlers. Flora took a back seat to fauna; the first laws to protect animals were as early as 1657 but plants had to wait 257 years to be given protected status. A report published by the Wildlife Society in 1977 showed that a survey revealed 60% of the Cape's fynbos had disappeared. The survey reported 36 extinct species, 1,259 plants threatened, 89 endangered and 110 listed as rare. The Cape floral kingdom is the smallest in area but the richest in species of the world's floral kingdoms, and its staggering variety of plants faced multiple threats. In ecological terms, all things are connected and the plant life needs to be protected for the well-being of all other creatures.

The bontebok was saved from extinction not by the authorities but by some Cape farmers who provided a protected area for the survivors. The Bontebok National Park was finally established near Bredasdorp but this proved to be unsuitable and the park was relocated to an area near Swellendam. Here the animals have thrived to the point that they are no longer listed as endangered. The gnu (black wildebeest) was also saved by the actions of a few farmers, who began protecting two herds of 300 animals in the Kroonstad district. The 1930s witnessed the designation of not only the Bontebok park but also the Cape of Good Hope Nature Reserve, Addo National Park, the Mountain Zebra National Park and the Kalahari Gemsbok National Park in the far northern Cape.

South Africa was making giant strides in making up for the mistakes of the early days. Although many of these positive steps were initiated by the public and the non-government bodies with the authorities becoming involved reluctantly, the South African government eventually took control and has since established a fine reputation in managing wildlife.

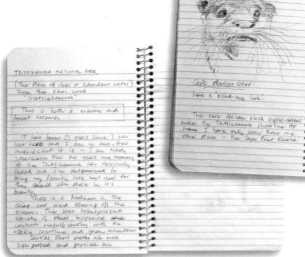

The Tsitsikamma coast at the mouth of Storms River

Extract from the notes above:
Tsitsikamma National Park (The place of clear or abundant water) from the Khoi word Sietsiekamma...

This is both a marine and forest reserve.

It has been 21 years since I was here and I am in awe. How magnificent it is – I am truly speechless ... there is a freshness in the crisp, cool wind blowing off the ocean.

Extract from the notes above:
Cape clawless Otter have a 'blind-eye look'.

...I did not see the shy blue duiker but heard the Kuysua Lourie on several occasions. The Lourie call is familiar to me as we had them where I grew up in Zimbabwe's eastern highlands.

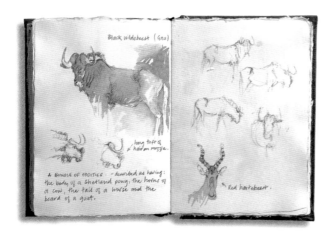

The notes on the left read:
Black wildebeest (gnu): A Bundle of Oddities – described as having: the body of a Shetland pony, the horns of a cow, the tail of a horse and the beard of a goat.

KING CHEETAH

Much was written about the king cheetah and the only evidence that it existed was a skin owned by a man in Palapye, Botswana. Speculation was that it was a subspecies of the common cheetah and the search was on to find a live animal. Within a few weeks of one another, two were born in captivity; one at the De Wildt Cheetah Research Station in the Transvaal and another at a small private park on the outskirts of Port Elizabeth where I was living at the time. Being a frequent visitor to the park, I had the opportunity to see this animal first hand. The king cheetah is not a subspecies but an aberrant cheetah with an extra black pigment called abundism.

When Addo National Park was proclaimed in 1931, only 11 elephant were left to rebuild a population. In 1954 the fencing of the park was completed, a massive undertaking that would ensure the protection of the Addo elephant.

Addo is also important for its buffalo herd. The Addo buffalo are the only survivors of the once huge herds of the Cape. Because of their isolation over a long period, they are disease free and provide an important pool for translocating stock to other reserves and parks.

The black rhino was introduced (Addo being the former home of the southern subspecies) using animals from Tanzania. This turned out to be a mistake as the black rhino in East Africa are the northern subspecies and do not belong in the south. Mixing subspecies is regarded as undesirable and this relocation effort, although done with good intentions, should not have taken place.

Conflicts with man made the Addo elephant dangerous and mistrustful. This attitude had to be dissolved before visitors could be allowed in the park. In its early days, the park was not popular as the nervous animals and the dense bush made for disappointing viewing. The park adopted a policy of feeding the elephant oranges to attract them to the fence, thereby providing an opportunity to see them. Anthony Hall-Martin, a biologist who went on to become a renowned elephant expert, began his research on the Addo elephant in 1976. He had to overcome the aggressive behaviour of

Addo elephants, the most southern herd after the Knysna group, survived because of the dense bush in the Eastern Cape, which was known to be a hunter's hell. Impenetrable in parts, this dense, thorny country became the refuge of about 140 elephant. Unfortunately there was no water in this natural refuge and the elephant had to drink at the nearby

farms under the protection of darkness. This brought them into conflict with people and in 1919 Major P. J. Pretorius was commissioned to eradicate the elephants. In 11 months he shot 120 animals. The slaughter provoked much public sympathy and with the help of the Wildlife Society, the hunt was called off with 16 elephant remaining.

Addo elephant are no different from other elephant in enjoying a mudbath.

these animals which he did by facing down a number of charges. Once they learnt to accept him and his vehicle, other vehicles were also gradually accepted and in due course visitors could safely enter the park.

Artistically I found the Addo elephants to be distinctive. Although these animals are not considered a subspecies, the cows are tuskless and the young are much fatter than those found elsewhere and have unusually thick legs.

MOUNTAIN ZEBRA NATIONAL PARK

Mountain Zebra National Park, like the Bontebok Park, was established to protect a single species, in this case the Cape mountain zebra. At the time the park was proclaimed, there were six animals – five stallions and one mare – within the designated area. By 1950 only two stallions remained in the park and fewer than 100 animals elsewhere. The future of the park and the zebra looked bleak, but a private donation of 11 animals and the purchase of a farm neighbouring the park brought the population to 55.

Early on, the size of the park was only large enough for 200 zebra, well below the accepted figure of 500 to ensure a viable genetic pool of the species in one geographical location. It is good news that in the last few years the park has acquired additional land, increasing from 6,536 hectares to 15,543 hectares. With this expansion the future of this rare animal at least looks secure.

The map on the left shows the terrain of the Mountain Zebra National Park as it is today.

Mountain zebra

A Cape mountain zebra is touched by the late afternoon sun in the Mountain Zebra National Park.

Gnu

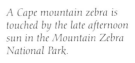

Kwazulu-Natal, on the eastern side of South Africa, is the traditional home of the Zulu nation. The Zulu today maintain a warrior air, inherited from the legendary King Chaka who ruled this land with an iron fist and fought all comers, including the might of the British army. Zululand, as the northern part of Natal is known, has game reserves with their own special character. Animals that are rarely seen elsewhere are common here. Both the exceedingly rare southern black rhino and the white rhino are found in substantial numbers in the Mkuzi, Umfolozi and Hluhluwe game reserves. The latter two and the St Lucia conservation areas are among the oldest existing wildlife sanctuaries to be proclaimed on the African Continent.

Umfolozi has been a battleground in the fight against Nagana, or sleeping sickness, carried by the tsetse fly. The first step attempted was to kill their hosts. Masses of animals, especially the zebra, were slaughtered. But it was found that after this radical project had been completed, the fly had increased. Trapping the tsetse was then the order of the day and for some time this method appeared to be working. Another flare-up of the fly between 1939 and 1943 resulted in the death of 60,000 head of cattle. The slaughter that followed saw 30,000 wild animals killed in a three-month period. Spraying was then introduced and the tsetse fly was finally eradicated from the Umfolozi and Hluhluwe area.

KIM DONALDSON

Serval cat

The map above is of the Mkuzi Game Reserve. The reserve provides two hides alongside the waterholes which allow close study of visiting animals.

The visitor today is unaware of this turbulent time. The parks are well established and at peace with their neighbours. It is particularly rewarding in light of the rhinos' plight elsewhere in Africa to see these wonderful beasts in numbers in the wild.

For several years I lived in Natal and took every opportunity to visit these parks. The Mkuzi Game Reserve was my favourite because of two hides – Bube and Msinga. At these hides, which are situated right next to waterholes, I could study animals up close, sketching away to my heart's content. Other hide visitors were of the educated sort and graciously left me alone. Many professional and serious amateur wildlife photographers frequented the hides and strict silence was broken only by the click of camera shutters. I was initially introduced to this place by the remarkable paintings of my friend and fellow artist Dino Paravano. Here he captured the shy nyala as it came to drink, the late afternoon light casting long shadows on the ground as the warm rays of the sun danced on the flanks of the animals. With patience one can see a tremendous amount in one sitting. I always felt sorry for the impatient people who stopped by for a few minutes before hurrying off somewhere else, only to miss a wonderful opportunity. As soon as they left something exciting inevitably unfolded, like the arrival of a rhino with its calf.

A nyala ewe in the thick thornveld characterizing much of Mkuzi.

The nyala is common in this area. Scarcely any other African animal has such a difference in colouring and size between the male and the female of the species. The male is the most handsome animal; dark chocolate with vertical white lines, it has a long mane and a strip of long white hair along its back. The horns are fairly long and spiral. The ewe is much smaller and hornless; it has similar vertical lines on its body but it is a rich red sienna that positively glows in the sunlight. The young are Africa's version of Bambi and they can be found on their own at a remarkably young age. Nyala inhabit dense bush, so the best place to see them is from the waterhole hides when they have to come out into the open to drink.

One tends to associate certain areas with specific animals, birds and vegetation. For me, Mkuzi is nyala country although it has many other animals to offer. The Umfolozi and Hluhluwe game reserves are rhino country. Often I visit specific wildlife areas to study specific animals. Rhino were relatively common in several parks in the 1970s when I started painting so I did not go anywhere with the sole intention of seeing them. One came across them without much effort at all. Times have changed. It has become rare indeed to find either black or white rhino. The parks in Zululand are the exception, which makes them important not only to the continued survival of the species but to me as an artist. I now visit these areas to see these wonderfully prehistoric creatures. Several thousand southern white rhino have been distributed from Zululand to other parts of southern Africa, East Africa and zoos and animal parks throughout the world. Most of these reintroductions in South Africa have been successful and the white rhino's future in South Africa looks good. Translocations to other African countries have not had the results hoped for and poaching continues to make the overall future for the species doubtful elsewhere.

Private game ranches are popping up throughout much of Africa and Kwazulu-Natal has its fair share. These are designed to make money and cater to those that want a quick bush vacation along with personal service, luxury accommodation and fine dining. These private parks, although commercially motivated, are a

Red-billed oxpeckers.

Two species common to Mkuzi are the warthog and the red-billed oxpecker.
Animals tolerate these birds as they rid their hosts of insect parasites.

Black rhino

White rhino

Burchell's zebra take their daily drink at a Mkuzi waterhole.

good thing for wildlife in general as they usually have sound management of the land and provide an additional protected and controlled place for the wildlife. I have on occasion utilized these private areas as their guides tend to get to know the animals and their habits. For example one can spend weeks looking for an elusive animal such as the leopard in the wild, whereas the operators in a private reserve can zero in on one that they know frequents a certain range and can

thus offer an almost instant opportunity to see what you are looking for.

The bush in many of these Zululand parks is fairly thick, with the result that game and bird viewing can be time consuming. As in most wild places, and this is especially true here, waterholes therefore provide the easiest viewing. For anyone with a restricted time frame, the private operations are the best bet as they often provide the whole African experience.

KRUGER NATIONAL PARK

Kruger National Park has an unequalled diversity of animals, birds and plant life. It is capable of accommodating 650,000 visitors a year and is the only national park in Africa that generates enough income to be self-sufficient. If size is the factor used to denote importance, Kruger is in the top ten national parks in the world. It occupies 7,523 square miles (19,485 sq. km) and is 206 miles (332 km) from north to south. The park is bigger than Israel and home to 2,000 forms of vegetation, 146 mammal and 490 bird species. All-weather tourist roads crisscross the park for over 1,400 miles (2,200 km) giving ample opportunity to see the wonderful variety it has to offer. Numerous walking trails have been introduced, allowing one a more natural experience.

To do Kruger park justice, many more pages would be required. Trying to cover it in a short chapter is like trying to capture the magnitude of the Grand Canyon in paint on postcard-size canvas.

Six major rivers flow through the park but in times of severe drought they can dry up to just a few waterholes. The animals must move or die. Such droughts are a natural occurrence, and they can take a heavy toll on habitat, so that the wildlife faces a double problem of finding enough to eat as well as finding water. Now that the Kruger is fenced and the larger animals cannot leave in search of water or grazing, human intervention is needed to check the numbers of some species in order to ensure the well-being of all. The area is no longer just a sector of the far larger wilderness that existed long ago.

Management is based heavily on scientific research, aimed at compensating for the fact that the wildlife is now restricted, but nevertheless aimed at exercising a policy of minimal interference. A programme of culling elephant and buffalo to control their populations within the park – because these are the species that can impact upon habitat most severely – has its critics.

Young giraffe

Circumstances adjacent to the park produce concerns as well. Water pollution in rivers that flow through the Kruger is a problem, and fires can move in across the boundaries. The park is divided into 400 management blocks, separated by tourist roads, firebreaks and patrol roads. The maze of such non-tourist roads totals some 4,000 kilometres. On one visit a number of years ago, I somehow ended up on one of these firebreak roads that seemed never-ending. I was not concerned about being lost, as the mapping within the park is excellent and I knew I would eventually come to another road or signpost that would enlighten me as to my whereabouts; but I was concerned about being caught by a park ranger who would not believe I had lost my way. Visitors also dislike travelling on the dirt roads and traffic on these secondary roads can be minimal.

As with most places I frequent, I have acquired favourite spots where I like to spend my time. One day at an off-the-beaten-track waterhole, I fell asleep while waiting for the game to come to drink. Something woke me and I had that curious feeling that I was not alone; turning to look behind me, I found myself face to face with a baboon sitting on my back seat. With a loud yell from me and a squeal from the baboon, we both exited the truck in a split second, to end up facing each other from opposite sides of the vehicle. Recovering quickly, I looked around, more concerned that someone had witnessed this ludicrous event than I was for the baboon. The

With sad, melancholy, wondering eyes, the giraffe seems to peer into the world of the present where there is room for it no longer. C. G. Schillings, photographer & hunter, 1907.

Tall blondes

baboon, however, which had been rummaging through my garbage bag in the back of my truck, had not made the mistake of leaving behind his prize in the flurry. After this episode, I became a little more tolerant of trash in the park as I realized it was not always ignorant visitors who were responsible.

The biggest attraction is the predators. Kruger is an exceptional place to see leopards, which live here in unusually high numbers. All the other predators can readily be found, including the African wild dog. There are more lions per head

of game in the park than anywhere else in Africa. The impala with their rich red-brown bodies are abundant and Kruger supports between 100,000 and 150,000 of these beautiful animals. They are the staple food for most of the predators and act as a buffer for the less common roan and sable antelope.

However, for me, Kruger is tusker country. This is the home of the 'Magnificent Seven' – seven elephant bulls with exceptionally large tusks that were made even more famous by my friend Paul Bosman, an artist who faithfully captured them in their natural environment. Some of these bulls were seldom seen by visitors as they lived away from the heavily travelled areas but some were very visible and could be watched on a regular basis. The bull named Shingwedzi was well-known for his placid nature and his tolerance for visitors and I have spent quite some time with him. He was often joined by younger bulls, which is the way knowledge is passed from one generation to the next. I was sometimes perplexed that visitors spent so little time with an animal as extraordinary as Shingwedzi, stopping for just a few moments before hurrying off in search of better things. Perhaps they did not realize the greatness that was before them.

The ultimate scenario for me as an artist is to be able to watch elephants in the vicinity of that other African giant, the baobab

Passing through

tree. The baobab (*Adansonia digitata*) and the elephant are symbolic of the lowveld; a semi-arid savannah periodically subject to drought. I love this place but I sense that when I paint it, my feelings for it are lost on some people. I suppose it is not love at first sight and one has to develop an attraction for this hot, dry, scruffy bushveld and its host of biting insects. This is the land of the giants, where life is harsh and survival is an accomplishment. Baobab trees routinely live hundreds of years, some even topping 3,000 years. Their enormous size and unusual design have earned a place in African mythology as a tree planted upside down by an angry god.

Old Kruger bull

The notebook on the right contains a list of the 'Magnificent Seven.' These are the largest elephant tusks that have been recorded in the Kruger National Park. The largest elephant is Kambaku (Big elephant) whose combined tusks weighed over 280 lbs.

Kruger tuskers

The magnificent seven of the Kruger National Park

JOÃO – (Portuguese for John)   L. 50-55 kg   (110-120 lbs)   Both tusks
                                    R. 41-45 kg   (90-100 lbs)   broken in 1984
NDLULAMITHI – (Taller than trees) L. 64½ kg.   (142 lbs)
KAMBAKU – (Big elephant)   R. 57 kg   (126 lbs)
                                    L 63½ kg   (140 lbs)   Heaviest ivory
MAFUNYANE – (Irritable one)   L 64 kg   (141 lbs)
                                    R 55 kg   (121 lbs)
DZOMBO – (Named after river)   L 55 kg   (121 lbs)
                                    R 55½ kg   (122 lbs)
SHAWU – (Named after Shawu area) L 56½ kg   (125 lbs)
                                    R 52½ kg   (116 lbs)   longest ivory –
SHINGWEDZI – (Named after river)   L 50½ kg   (112 lbs)   over 3 m. (10 feet)
                                    R 58 kg   (128 lbs)
                                    L 47 kg   (104 lbs)

Leopard. Winter morning in the Kruger Park.

Light to an artist is as important as pollen to a bee; without it the mixture is just not honey. A photographer may like cloudy, overcast weather because it gives the subject definition. A sunny day on the other hand casts shadows and creates too much contrast so that detail is lost. However, one man's loss is another man's gain and those sunny days are the source of the nuances so eagerly sought by the artist. The warm light of the first rays of dawn, for example, provides a wonderful contrast to the cool colours of the early morning. In trying to capture this in a painting, one is stretched to render both cool and warm colours in the same image, to convey the magic.

Early winter is the best time in Kruger as the days are cool and generally cloudless. However the weather towards the end of winter (August) can be very cloudy and I have had many grey days at this time of the year.

S-39 (N)

TIMBAVATI
REST-SPOT.

S-40

MASALA

H7

MAROELA
CAMP

ORPEN
GATE

MZANZENE

✳ LEOPARD SIGHTING.

Impala share the shade provided by a sparse acacia tree.

To
LETABA

HI-4

SATARA
CAMP

HI-3

To SKUKUZA.

Heavy, overcast weather moves in from the coast, blocking out the sun for days. Besides the usual sunshine, winter is good for game viewing as this is the dry season and the animals congregate at the waterholes. Game is also easier to see because the grass and leaf cover is more sparse. Although I have made many visits to Kruger at different times of the year, I have longed to spend a whole year there. One would need at least that much time to get the full benefit of the seasons and to see all that Kruger has to offer. We unfortunately live in a society where we make things difficult for ourselves and often prevent ourselves from doing the simple things that are worth doing. I am as guilty as the next person and always seem to have some pressing reason not to slip away and spend an extended time in the park.

A leopard, rarely seen out in the open during daylight hours, pauses as it listens to the barking of a distant baboon.

Leopard (Panthera pardus)

Kruger is possibly the best place to see the elusive leopard. Not only are they plentiful but they are also tolerant of tourist vehicles and readily use the roads to patrol their territories. Both males and females have clearly defined ranges. The male territories overlap those of the females, so that mating can take place, but do not intrude upon the space of other males. Kruger has ideal vegetation and abundant food sources for leopards to thrive, and their population density has attracted the attention of scientists. From my experience, I would estimate that it requires an average of fourteen days of game viewing to see a leopard in the wild. A really good encounter rather than a quick glimpse takes a lot more luck and hard work. But Kruger and the surrounding private parks are the exception. I have had numerous leopard sightings in this eastern section of South Africa which have been of paramount importance to me as the leopard is one of my favourite animals to paint.

Several years ago at Skukuza camp in Kruger, I had the good fortune to meet Harry Manners, the author of *Kambaku*. Harry is a man of the old school who earned his living in the early days hunting for ivory. I spent a memorable evening with him, eagerly listening to every word as with my encourgement, he recalled his experiences of an Africa that is no more. At times like this I believe I was born into the wrong generation. Today we rely on places like the Kruger Park, for the great wild areas of yesteryear have succumbed to human expansion. Rules must now govern the visitors and protect this wilderness; gone is the freedom that Harry had. But even so there is no question that this area is as good as it gets.

The richest part of the park for sheer animal numbers is the large central plain. Before the erection of a fence on the western boundary of the park in the early 1960s, the herds of wildebeest migrated, similar to movements in the Kalahari and on the Serengeti plains but on a smaller scale. One of the larger camps, Satara, is situated in the middle of this plain and gives one easy access to explore the area. An early start can give you the opportunity to see buffalo at dawn as they stiffly rise and stretch out their ample bodies, still cold from cool night air. There is no hurry in their movements as they slowly gather and begin moving off to graze on the plains. I had one of my most successful game-viewing days in the area immediately surrounding Satara.

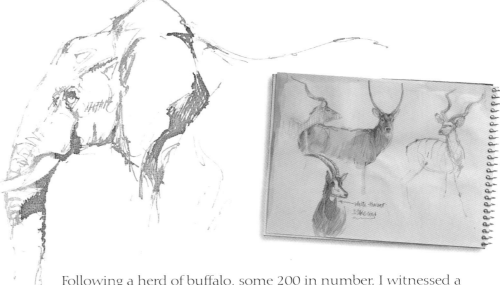

Following a herd of buffalo, some 200 in number, I witnessed a large pride of lions go through their manoeuvres to separate an animal from the protection of the herd. The process of attack and retreat was repeated over the course of an hour before one lioness tackled an adult bull. The cats were driven off by the herd, which then retreated in panic. The lions were successful in the end, bringing down one of the buffalo. A free-for-all ensued at the kill as the lions that had cooperated in the hunt went through their normal change of character, snarling and lashing out at one another to get a share of the kill. One of the lionesses that had been injured during the hunt limped up to the carcass on three legs but was driven off by the others. This most likely was the end for her unless she quickly recovered and could successfully take her place in future hunts and be strong enough to secure her share of the kill.

Moving on from there, I came across an adult male leopard lying in the shade of an acacia tree next to the road. After a while he casually sauntered off, walking parallel to the road before disappearing into the thicker bush. A few hours later, I was blessed with encountering a pair of cheetah. Not only was this the first time I had seen Africa's three large cats on one day but all my sightings had been exceptional.

On the way back to camp at the end of the day, I met the buffalo herd I had watched earlier on. The buffalo bull that had first been attacked bore the evidence of his encounter with the lions; long bloody claw marks covered his back and flanks and he was

Sable montage

SABLE ANTELOPE ~
hippotragus niger

Note blue reflection from the sky.

Note the heavy mane.

Females are a dark chestnut. Legs and upper thigh are a lighter ochre.

South Africa 70c
POST OFFICE

Males are much darker than females and calfs. Field impression is startling in comparison to other antelope which blend with their surroundings. Bulls have a glossy black appearance with contrasting white faces, belly and rump.

dripping blood from his face and nose. I made the mistake of telling another visitor how strong buffalo are and that it would probably survive the ordeal. The following day I learnt that the bull had died in the night, proving that it is best not to pretend to know what one can't know.

Included in the vast variety of animals is the relatively rare roan antelope. Roan numbers are of such concern to the park that the animals are annually immunized against anthrax. Their close relative the sable antelope, which for me is the most

magnificent antelope in Africa, is more numerous than the roan but equally difficult to see.

Kruger National Park has set the standard in wilderness management for the rest of Africa. Other parks could benefit in learning from mistakes and successes here. It is one of the few wildlife areas on the continent that I am not concerned about for I know the Kruger is in good hands and that all its creatures will be protected. The more I travel in Africa, the more I realize what an exceptional place this is.

ROAN ANTELOPE
(hippotragus equinus)

WET SEASON
CONDITION

DRY SEASON
CONDITION

Roan do not adapt
well to changes to
their habitat. Coupled
with a reliance on water,
the roan is on the
Endangered Species list.

The closely related Sable
(hippotragus niger) is tough
and hardy and is more
adaptable.

SOUTHERN RACE VARIATION. IS MORE GREY THAN THE OTHER
COLOURATION TYPES (Western, East African & Angolan race)

Roan antelope

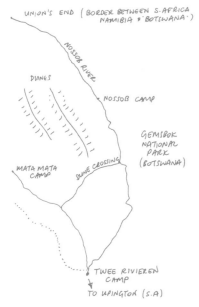

UNION'S END (BORDER BETWEEN S. AFRICA NAMIBIA & BOTSWANA)

NOSSOB RIVER

DUNES

NOSSOB CAMP

GEMSBOK NATIONAL PARK (BOTSWANA)

MATA MATA CAMP

DUNE CROSSING

TWEE RIVIEREN CAMP

TO UPINGTON (S.A)

In southern Africa the Gemsbok Park has an open border with Botswana and a conservation area that ranks as one of the largest in the world.

Cheetah portraiture

KALAHARI GEMSBOK NATIONAL PARK

Kalahari Gemsbok National Park is a vast, dry finger of land that points northwards between Namibia and Botswana to Union's End – possibly the remotest place in southern Africa. Even though this park is a long way from just about anywhere and longer en route to Namibia as it was when the Mata Mata border to the north was operational, it certainly has its dedicated followers who make the arduous journey. This effort is rewarded by the unique beauty of the park, which is very different from the other wild areas in South Africa. It does in reality give the impression of belonging to Namibia or Botswana rather than the Cape.

The Kalahari Gemsbok Park shares a common and open border with Botswana's Gemsbok National Park – unimpeded by fences and man-made restrictions, the two countries have a conservation area that ranks as one of the largest in the world.

This wilderness falls within the Kalahari – a belt of sand that stretches from the Cape to the southern borders of Zambia and Angola. The Kalahari, which

The notebook above reads: Red hartebeest – rather ordinary until they run in their graceful gait.

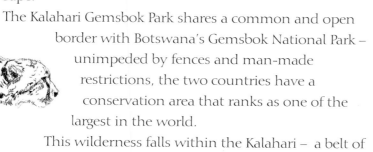

A sociable weavers' nest – broken branches are common from the sheer weight.

The name Kalahari originates from the word Kgalagadi which means wilderness. It is extremely dry and there is no natural surface water. The oryx or gemsbuck, which are known locally as gemsbok, inhabit this 'desert' as they have the ability to survive without water. The gemsbuck get most of their moisture from plants such as the tsamma (Citrullus lanatus), which is a melon.

Gemsbuck, Kalahari
Gemsbok National Park

Springbuck

covers most of Botswana, is possibly the largest untamed and unknown wilderness paradise left in Africa. The Kalahari Gemsbok National Park is the most travelled part in this southern sector but this is a relative term and by Kruger Park and East African park standards, there are few visitors.

This area has no surface water and has subsequently benefitted by having little for people to covet. On a map the two rivers that define the park give a false impression as only in years of exceptional rain do they hold any surface water. Man has intervened and artificial watering points are now in place along the two river beds. Even so, the larger herbivorous animals of the Kalahari are nomadic, which makes the cooperation between the two parks vitally important.

Life is precarious at best. Summer daytime temperatures regularly exceed 40° C (104° F) with the ground heating to a scorching 70° C (158° F). In sharp contrast, winter nights drop below freezing and frost can quickly blacken the grass, making life even more difficult. The only shelter from the sun is the shade of the camel-thorn and shepherd trees. But in this shade lurk nasty little creatures called tampans. Triggered by the exhaled carbon dioxide from man or beast, these ticks attach themselves to a host in hordes and an attack by these swarms can leave festering ulcerations that may weaken or kill animals.

The most common antelope here are the gemsbuck, blue wildebeest and red hartebeest. The largest of them all, eland, are predominantly browsers and their presence in the park is governed by the availability of food. The elephant, buffalo, giraffe and rhino commonly associated with wild Africa do not make their home in this area. This in no way lessens the enjoyment for the visitor as the park has so much else to offer. The graceful springbuck is ever present and the magnificent gemsbuck, which has a unique blood-cooling system in its nostrils that prevents it from getting too hot, is a joy to see in its natural habitat. Animals adapted to hot, dry country fare best in the Kalahari and although most of the species found here can go without water, they will readily drink when water is available.

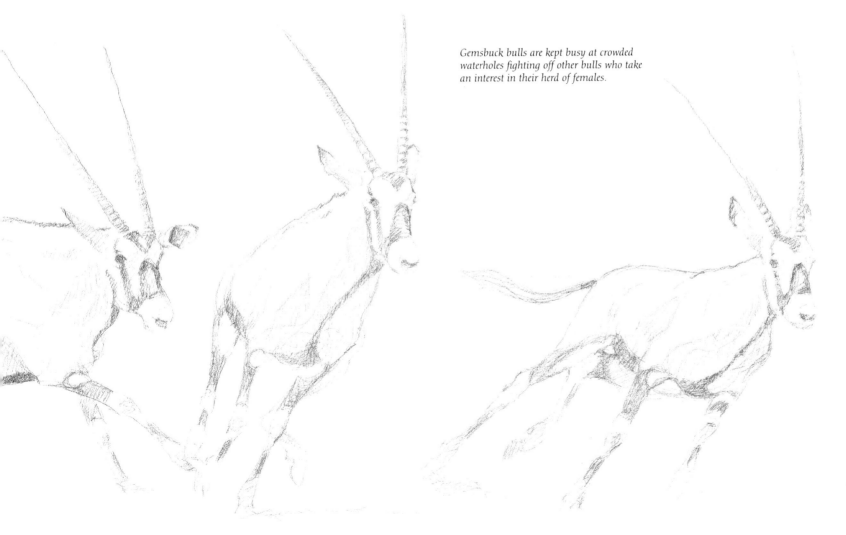

Gemsbuck bulls are kept busy at crowded waterholes fighting off other bulls who take an interest in their herd of females.

White-backed vultures take to the air with a little difficulty.

Meercat

Grou

Rear view - troop on the run

Extracts from the notebooks on the left:
Kalahari Gemsbok National Park.

...The drive from Uppington to G.N.P. southern gate and campsite was very interesting and I would like to spend more time in the area when I next get a chance.

Today was pretty spectacular!!! Cheetah, lion, gemsbok, wildebeest, eland, red hartebeest, bat-eared fox, suricate and of course springbuck – saw them all. Also found a leopard kill in a thorn tree but no leopard.

I spent the whole day today with a cheetah mother and her three cubs and was rewarded by seeing her catch and kill a springbuck. She then pulled the springbuck a few hundred yards to a camel-thorn tree that had a lot of broken branches. This provided shade and visual protection – both essential.

Ecologists are monitoring the long-term effects of supplying permanent watering points. Some species, like the wildebeest, are not migrating as they did before the boreholes were in place. The Kalahari functioned before these boreholes were introduced and other than making it easier for visitors to see the animals, they are unnecessary.

The Kalahari is a vital refuge for a rather ugly but ecologically fascinating animal, the brown hyaena. Classified as endangered and heavily persecuted by farmers, it may not have a population large enough to guarantee its long-term future.

Because of the harshness of the habitat the famous Kalahari lion, another of the park's residents, have territories in excess of one thousand square kilometres. Large prey is not always available, requiring them to feed on smaller animals. Mark and Delia Owens studied this remarkable animal in central Botswana and I highly recommend their book *Cry of the Kalahari*.

Kalahari Gemsbok National Park also has numerous other

Leopard portraiture

Gemsbuck herd

Studies of the Oryx family.

Beisa Oryx - (oryx beisa)
black markings are slimmer
than the gemsbuck. Note
there are none on the hind
legs.

Gemsbuck (Gemsbok)
is known as the southern oryx.
It is only found in S.W. Africa.

An injured horn at a
young age will often
grow on a different line.
This is fairly common and
if the bend is severe, the
horn will grow into the neck or
body causing
injury or
sometimes even
death.

predators. It has a healthy population of cheetah that are easily seen in the open terrain along the dry river beds. Leopard, African wild cat and the caracal, although harder to find, are also residents of the park.

This place is a stern reminder of the realities of the natural world, where only the strongest survive. Predators and scavengers may at first appear to rule but the weather shows no favouritism and all creatures of the Kalahari are at its mercy.

South Africa is by far the most modern and industrialized country on the African continent. It is a leader in sophisticated wildlife management and research and provides safe havens for several endemic species. Yet it also has such remote places as the red Kalahari dunelands with their specialized ecology, sturdy survivors, and fiercely rarefied pleasures for the artist. What could be more different from the fynbos of the rocky Cape shores than the sandy emptiness and open vistas of the Kalahari? As with so many other facets of South Africa, when it comes to wild areas, contrast is the key.

K.M. DONALDSON

Raptor montage

The Kalahari lions are much larger than those found elsewhere in southern Africa. East Africa's lions, although having spectacular manes, are the smallest in body mass.

Mature black maned lion. — Kransbrak. (North of Twee Riveren) - Nossob Valley. k. G.N.P.

The Kalahari lions are much larger than those found elsewhere in southern Africa. E. Africa's lions, although having spectacular manes, are the smallest in body mass.

decades been a shining star of stability on a continent of political turmoil. The country and its people benefit from mineral wealth and a large cattle industry. Botswana is blessed with an astonishing natural phenomenon, a product of the southernmost part of the great rift system: the inland delta of the Okavango. Most of Botswana is covered by the Kalahari sands, a dry country of plants and animals that have evolved to survive with a minimum of water. Yet in the middle of

BOTSWANA

this desert lies a massive, life-giving delta, an area of exceptional beauty and considerable herds of game. Water is a precious commodity in a land this dry, and much of what happens in Botswana revolves around it. The Okavango is the crown jewel, playing a major financial role for the country through photographic tourism and hunting.

This fragile treasure with its maze of meandering channels covers about 6,200 square miles (1,600 sq. km).

Having a sense of humour helps make a safari more enjoyable!

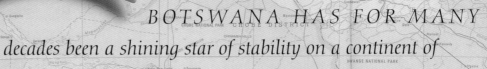

Giraffe at Nxai Pan

The Central Kalahari Game Reserve lies deep in the inhospitable centre of the country. Few people venture this far and access is difficult. This is where Mark and Delia Owens did their remarkable work on lions in Deception Valley. Unfortunately their criticism of the government's Kuke cattle fence, which prevented wildebeest from reaching their northern source of water during drought years and subsequently killed millions, had the pair unceremoniously thrown out of the country. These fences have been erected to control the spread of foot-and-mouth disease and to protect the growing cattle industry, but they have taken a heavy toll on wildlife and angered conservationists. Gemsbok National Park in the south-west has amalgamated with South Africa's Kalahari Gemsbok National Park to form the Kgalagadi Tranfrontier Park, the first of its kind in southern Africa. This zone has few human

Giraffe drinking

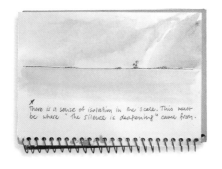

There is a sense of isolation in the scale. This must be where "the silence is deafening" came from.

inhabitants and does not face the pressures of growing human and cattle populations. Migration of wild herds is necessary to their survival and as old as time itself. The Makgadikgadi and Nxai Pan areas enjoy the benefit of having large herds of animals move in at certain times of the year. These movements still occur to a degree but on a much smaller scale than before the fences were erected. After exceptionally good rains, the shallow lake beds are covered by a sheet of water that can stretch for hundreds of miles. This attracts flamingoes in their thousands to feed on the crustaceans miraculously brought to life by the surface water in the salty pans. What can at times look like a place devoid of life is suddenly a hive of activity.

Ostrich move through the vast open plains as a mirage dances on the horizon.

Extracts from the notebooks on the left:
There is a sense of isolation in the scale. This must be where 'the silence is deafening' came from.

Nxai Pan and Kama-Kama Pan to the north is so different to the more popular areas such as the delta. Here you can almost hear yourself breathe.

I am always here at the end of winter and before the rains so have not witnessed the large zebra migrations to the area.

A tribute to Baines

*A herd of zebra kick up
clouds of dust in their panic.*

North of the main Nata/Maun road lie Nxai Pan and the Baines Baobabs. Many visitors hurrying to reach their main goal of the Okavango Delta and the Chobe make the mistake of not stopping in this area. The Nxai and Makgadikgadi pans are a small part of a larger system that was once an enormous lake. An illusion of water is usually all that remains as mirages dance in the hazy heat. Time and tectonics have changed the balance: between them, the effects of crustal shifts and warming climate seem to be responsible for the drying of what were once very large lakes. I take every opportunity to stop by and walk in the footsteps of Thomas Baines. Baobab trees are astounding at the best of times and even more so when surrounded by miles of treeless terrain on all sides.

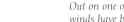

Extracts from the notebooks above:
Out on one of the bare pans today a dust storm hit me. The winds have been blowing pretty hard today – they are hot and uncomfortable. I wonder about early explorers and travellers like Thomas Baines – how difficult it must have been at times!

Baobabs were painted by Thomas Baines in 1862. His watercolour shows how little the close cluster of trees have changed in the past 130-odd years.

The notebook on the left reads:
Fronds at the top are green.
Fronds in the middle are ochre and hang down. Old fronds are stalks.

There are a lot of wild places that evoke a sense of utopia – of wildlife unfettered and primeval – but few evoke the sense of Eden as strongly as does the Okavango. One is taken aback to find a swamp within an ecosystem that has such low rainfall. It is a glittering jewel fed by waters from far away. Water flows in annually to renew the wonder. This African wetland wilderness is a place of creeping waters, forever advancing and receding in a perpetual cycle. My first visit was in the late 1970s when I spent a few days in Moremi Wildlife Reserve, some of which falls within the Okavango Delta. Early on, I lost most of my food to marauding baboons, which pillaged my meagre pantry. The public campsite offered little, and as no other campers were in residence, I had to make do with what little the baboons left

behind. This first visit did, however, make me want to come back. The delta is huge and difficult to negotiate. Even though I have subsequently travelled to and stayed in many different parts of the delta, I still feel I have barely come to know it.

The Okavango is home to the rare sitatunga, a shy antelope that inhabits the dense reedbeds lining the more permanent waterways of the swamp. The mokoro, a dugout made by local residents, is the traditional means of transportation and surpasses any modern craft for practical delta travel. The balance and control a mokoro poler has are remarkable, given that the dugout rides only a few inches above the water.

The 'arrival of the water' is an event that occupies the minds of residents of the delta and the safari town of Maun. Its arrival

Old buffalo bulls leave the herd, preferring the peaceful company of other old bulls.

The delta is home to a substantial population of elephant.

though is not dramatic but rather a matter of fingers of water slowly fanning out and constantly changing direction, seeking the lower ground. It seems all but miraculous to be standing on a hot, dry stretch of land that has not had any rain in six months, when out of the blue you encounter a growing puddle of cool, clear water. Most of the water that enters the swamp is lost to evaporation.

Travelling by light aircraft not only makes getting around much easier but it also gives one a different perspective of this marvellous place. The Okavango seems smaller and more fragile when seen from the air. Human settlements appear more frequent and safari camps visibly dot the main waterways. Moremi is unusual in that the park was initiated by the local Tswana people to protect their traditional land from outsiders. The park has no fences and animals are free to move between the swamps and the Chobe National Park. Chief's Island is the

Wild dog (Lycaon pictus)

A young dog becomes another
ROAD KILL.

most prominent land feature, almost entirely within the Moremi reserve. Game viewing does not come easy in this neck of the woods as the thick sand keeps you in four-wheel drive most of the time and road signs are often non-existent. Reedbuck, lechwe, waterbuck and sitatunga abound in the wetter regions. Chobe bushbuck and roan antelope can also be found in the drier sector. The wild dog has been extensively studied in the Moremi and surrounding areas by wildlife biologist John 'Tico' McNutt. He and his wife Lesley Boggs have written a book on the wild dog, *Running Wild*, exposing many misconceptions about the species.

The animal is threatened throughout Africa. Rabies, anthrax, and canine distemper have an alarming effect, destroying entire packs. Wild dogs require an enormous range and this brings them into conflict with resident predators and with livestock owners adjoining parks. This problem is increasing as the tsetse fly is eradicated. Reintroduced packs have not fared well for these reasons, and overall the species is more endangered than the rhino.

Moremi elephant move through a belt of palm trees touched by the setting sun.

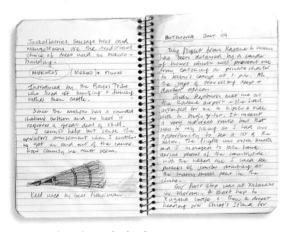

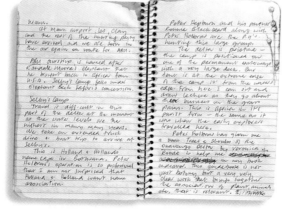

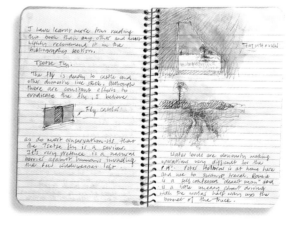

Extracts from the notebooks above:
Mokoros. Introduced by the Bayei tribe who lived off hunting and fishing rather than cattle. Since the Mokoro has a rounded shallow bottom and no keel it requires a great deal of skill.

Tsetse Fly. The fly is deadly to cattle and other domestic livestock. Although there are constant efforts to eradicate the fly, I believe as do most conservationists that the tsetse fly

is a saviour. Its very presence is a natural barrier against humans invading the few wildernesses left.

Lechwe (Kobus leche) only occur in areas of permanent water.

*C*ontrolled hunting in the delta draws big game hunters from all over the world. This area chiefly attracts those seeking the sitatunga and lechwe, which are not to be had elsewhere.

Permits and allocations to hunt lion have grown harder to get in recent years due to the work of Dereck and Beverly Joubert. While filming *Lions of Darkness* in Botswana, they noticed the repercussions the death of a dominant male had on the pride.

As a result of their findings, the Jouberts campaigned to have lion hunting in Botswana reduced. This presumably made them unpopular with the professional hunters. The issue of hunting is a subject that has been debated

Extract from the notebook above:
Elephant bulls make regular visits to the campsite. Their unhurried manner makes them ideal subjects to sketch. This can be done without binoculars because of their close proximity – sometimes they are too close.

for years and will always be controversial. Hunting brings in a healthy amount of foreign exchange – one hunter leaves behind a lot more money in Botswana than several non-hunters do. On the other hand, there are many more non-

hunting visitors than hunters. I believe there is room for both in the country's wild places, provided that there is enough monitoring and scientific work to keep everyone honest. Professional hunting outfits are heavily regulated, and the system in place may have its faults and many critics, but it does seem to work.

Lechwe are probably the animals people associate most closely with the delta region. They spend much of their time in small groups, feeding in belly-deep water. To retreat from intruders they bound away through the water in single file.

Accentuated by the late afternoon light, the white clay on the horns of this buffalo gives it a rather bizarre look.

CHOBE NATIONAL PARK

Chobe National Park at the northern edge of the country is home to a significant concentration of elephant. Anyone on a soapbox about how endangered the African elephant is needs a visit to the Chobe. But the herds are under some strain. Water is a scarce commodity, as in most of the country, and elephant obliterate food supplies where there is permanent water. Breeding herds thus have to travel substantial distances daily to get from their food sources to their water supply. Infant mortality, although high, has not slowed down the elephant population. The effects of overcrowding are noticeable: the area around Serondella in the northern part of the park looks like a moonscape in the dry season.

Chobe is not easy to get to unless you fly. The roads from the south are sandy and the going is hard. The first-time traveller is confounded by the lack of road signs but most of all by the way the roads branch in several directions, leaving you in a state of nervous indecision. There is some reason to be worried about this, as I found out when I accidentally drove into a military base in the middle of nowhere. The guard at the outpost was in an extremely agitated state after I almost rode over him. He held an AK47 to my head while my travelling companion made things worse by trying to be jovial. Military personnel in many parts of Africa can be hypersensitive and our situation was not good. Fortunately we were able to talk our way out of our predicament. After becoming more experienced in motoring in Botswana, you realize that all the tracks usually converge, and the crisis of a fork in the road is just a matter of selecting the freshest and best option.

Considering its size, Chobe has few visitors except up in the Serondella area, where access is easier. Most visitors do not venture far from the lodges. This is what attracts the likes of me to the park: you can spend days in Chobe and not see another person. A few years ago I was travelling a remote area on the eastern side of the park when I noticed someone running into the road ahead of me. He turned out to be a cook from Belgium, of all things. His hired safari truck had broken down six days earlier, leaving him stranded until I came along. I am always a little amused by my irritation when I encounter other people in the bush after I have begun to think of it as my own. Such isolation is difficult to find, which makes it sweet and precious when you do find it.

Extract from the notebook above:
September. The rain has been falling heavily all day but the elephant continue their daily ritual of drinking at the waterhole. This is the start of the 'good season' when food becomes more plentiful.

B O T S W A N A
The water saga —

Nogatsaa waterhole is sometimes awkward to get at!

At a previously productive, artificial waterhole, south of Nogatsaa, an elephant bull sloshes around in the mud, searching for drinkable water.

Savuti pump pan has a steady supply of fresh water. The overflow pool is however a muddy, urine-laden slug.

Elephant make watering points by digging in riverbeds that have no surface water. This benefits other creatures too.

Elephant can readily smell underground water and do pose a problem in some places where they share 'space' with humans by digging up and breaking underground water pipes.

Extract from the notebook on the left:
Botswana. The water saga. Savuti pump pan has a steady supply of fresh water. The overflow pool is however a muddy, urine-laden slug.

Elephant make watering points by digging in riverbeds that have no surface water. This benefits other creatures too.

Elephant can readily smell underground water and do pose a problem in some places where they share 'space' with humans by digging up and breaking underground water pipes.

Chobe is divided into three main sections, their circumstances inevitably influenced by the water factor. The northern zone has the permanent Chobe River as its lifeline. Linyanti in the north-west is fed by the Linyanti River and the third area, Savuti, survives without the help of the fickle Savuti channel, which stopped flowing in 1981 after a history of alternating periods of flow and no flow. The Savuti vlei was once a marsh fed by the Savuti channel. Underground faulting and subtle elevational changes deriving from crustal movement seem to be responsible for the on-again, off-again nature of the channel over geological time.

The vlei, however, remains a major attraction to large herds, especially zebra, which migrate into the Savuti annually. The animals that remain through the dry season rely on water artificially pumped to the surface. Unfortunately, even this supply fails occasionally and it is pitiful to see confused animals standing around in forlorn hope. If we take it upon ourselves to establish such watering points, the least we can do is to be consistent about it. But the ways of Africa are harsh. Sometimes there is no fuel for the generator or the pump breaks down.

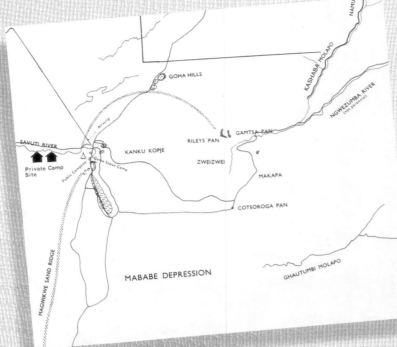

Savuti is not for sissies. The artificially maintained waterholes supply a focal point for predators and for game viewing. Here you can be witness to the agonizingly slow death of a baby elephant attacked by a pride of lions. Some of the scenes are so gruesome as to leave you wondering how much more you want to see. Lloyd Wilmot, a longtime and well-known resident of Savuti, told me that in the months prior to my September 1997 visit, the resident lion pride had killed several young elephant. The waterholes are dominated by bull elephants that remain in the Savuti all year round, often making it awkward for other animals to drink.

At his camp on the bank of the dry Savuti channel, Lloyd has a waterhole and bunker hide where bravehearts are encouraged to sit on top. While sitting there one night in the pitch dark with Lloyd and my travelling companions, Harold Bloch and South African Airways pilot Graham Smith, I got the giggles at Graham's nervous chatter after being caressed by an elephant's trunk. It is bizarre to be out in the bush surrounded by elephant bulls, so dark that you can't see your hand in front of your face, and to have an elephant touch and smell you.

The artist on top of Lloyd Wilmot's bunker hide

Within the montage (handwritten notes):

(females are 'ordinary' donkey-like looking)

The horns transform the male into a magnificent animal!

Waterbuck - kobus ellipsiprymnus largest of the 3 semi-aquatic antelope in the Delta. Less specialised than the sitatunga and the red lechwe the waterbuck (despite its name) has less to do with water, preferring the flood plains to the aquatic vegetation.

Only the males have horns — heavy, ringed, backward and upward curve

N.B. white ring
white muzzle and white stripe above the eyes.

Although the Delta appears to be an ideal habitat, the waterbuck is not as common as the lechwe.

Waterbuck montage

From the air, the Savuti vlei stands out as a large open grassland in contrast to the wooded surrounding countryside. I generally travel here in the late dry months of winter and early summer, so I have never witnessed the large herds of zebra and buffalo that gather here when conditions are wetter. In the dry season, everything moves at a snail's pace, the heat sapping the very soul from the land. The animals look thin and distressed, ribcages and hip bones evident.

Lioness

*Extract from the notebook
on the right:
6 lionesses are driven off
their kill by an almost
equal number of hyaena.
A lone male lion then took
control and the hyaenas
were driven off.*

King of the beasts

King of the beasts —

KIM DONALDSON

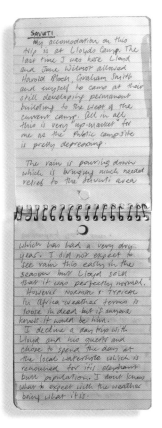

Extracts from the notebook below:
The rain is coming down hard and at an angle that forces me to keep my windows closed. This makes it a little difficult to do my sketching.

Yellow-billed kites frequent this pan and feed on the doves and sand grouse. Today they are really bombarding the doves. The elephant can vary the length of its trunk tremendously. In a relaxed state it can easily rest on the ground.

Extract from the notebook below:
Savuti has a varied past and although it has been supplied by an erratic watercourse it has been dry since 1981. Large herds of grazing animals are attracted to the Savuti when the annual rains fall and the marsh turns to green.

Extract from the notebook above:
The rain is pouring down which is bringing much needed relief to the Savuti area which has had a very dry year...

I decline a day trip ... and chose to spend the day at the local waterhole which is renowned for its elephant bull population...

Extract from the notebook above:
A Japanese film crew is also working at the waterhole. The bull elephant here are tolerant of vehicles and people.

Extract from the notebook on the right:
I got stuck today in a ravine between pump pan and the marsh. The banks were too steep and I slid into some deep sand. Fortunately another group of visitors happened my way and with the help of this group ... I was embarrassingly pulled out.

Tsessebe in the shade of an acacia tree on the edge of the Savuti vlei

Once I was present for the arrival of the rains. During the night a wind got up. Gusting and swirling, the wind attacked my tent for hours before the rain came. First it was hesitant, in single large drops that could be heard individually as they struck the canvas protecting me. The beat increased to a deafening roar as the rain pelted down in full fury. It was destined to be a restless night. Thunder rumbled and the lightning lit the sky. It is memorable indeed to spend a night in a tent during an African thunderstorm. It is equally memorable to go out into the bush early on the morning following the first rain of the season. The dust has been washed off the land, colours shine in the morning sun, and everything has a livelier gait and manner, as though cleansed by holy waters. The cycle of life resumes its vigour after the trials and hardships of dry times.

The lion and hyaena saga filmed by the Jouberts took place in this area and exposed how fiercely these predators must compete for survival. Both are numerous here. On one of my Savuti trips I was accompanied by a friend who was somewhat undone by his first night-time experience of being visited by a lion while sleeping in a tent. On our first night at the campsite, I was woken from a sound sleep by my friend's desperate whispers, accompanied by the rasping of a lion breathing just

Portrait of a king

Extract from the notebooks below:
The posture may look threatening but the forward-facing ears
and a tail lying flat on the ground suggest otherwise. This
attitude, however, can change in an instant.

A Savuti lion ignores a herd of zebra as he listens to a distant roar.

outside our tent. I assured him that they had no interest in us and we lay awake listening to them roaring late into the night. Remembering how frightening my first lion roar at night had been, I never made fun of him.

The following night we were visited by a far more dangerous animal – a bull elephant that had developed a nasty habit of taking what he wanted

from tents, occupied or not. We had been warned of this by another camper. Following his advice, when the elephant came to our tent (my friend who had given up sleeping let me know), I made a din by banging a pot on a metal table. Even in the face of this racket, the bull hesitated before breaking away from his intent, and I was left shaken by the experience. Moments later we could hear another camper going through the

Study for In Your Face

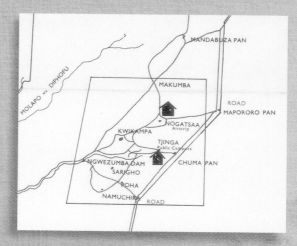

same self-preservation procedure. This elephant was eventually culled to protect visitors and locals.

Nogatsaa and Tchinga in the eastern side of the Chobe are a couple of artificial watering points installed to spread out the animals. Visitor facilities are non-existent, and few people bother with travelling here, but I fell in love with it. Here I have pitched my tent within 50 yards of the waterhole and have been surrounded by a continuous stream of elephant coming to drink. For three days in 1986 I had this place all to myself but for the elephant and other animals.

Several years later, in anticipation of a similar experience, I arrived at Nogatsaa to find that the Botswana army had moved in and taken over, driving their trucks into the waterhole to fill their drums. Thirsty elephant milled about. I hastily left. Just south of Nogatsaa on

Elephant share the precious water at Nogatsaa in north-central Botswana.

the road to Savuti, I was charged by two bull elephants. The unprovoked attack seemed completely out of character and I had to wonder if it had something to do with the human behaviour at the waterhole. It seemed contradictory to run into the military this way in peaceful Botswana; the best perspective I could muster was to chalk it up to Africa being ever the preserve of the unexpected.

Serondella is on the bank of the Chobe River. The flats alongside the river are like an oasis in a dry land and attract animals in great numbers. Waterbuck, puku and impala graze during the day in the company of baboons and warthog. Roan

antelope and the magnificent sable can be seen coming down from the nearby high ground to drink. Skittish and always wary, they gallop back to the safety of the thick bush at any disturbance.

The campsite at Serondella has a patchy record. When it became somewhat unsavoury, campers started spreading out beyond the campground. Baboons and other freeloaders robbed tents and garbage bins, and whereas one of the attractions of the area was the lack of regulation, it now became imperative to take matters in hand. It is a fine sight, at the end of the day when the air grows cooler, the light softens, and the atmosphere becomes

Botswana baobabs

Buffalo skull

Several dozen buffalo skulls and piles of bones littered the veld near the Chobe River leaving little doubt that a massacre had taken place.

Warthog montage

serene, to watch a large herd of elephant come down to drink. With luck, one may have managed to rinse off the dust, and now it's time to watch the elephants do likewise before they plaster themselves anew with mud. This is a good time to sit and be quiet, a good time to take in the sounds and smells of Africa. The baboons start to settle for the night in the trees above, occasional noisy squabbles issuing forth. The campfire burns and 'sundowners' welcome the finest time of the day.

At dawn you need to be up and running to catch the huge buffalo herd that has spent the night on the Chobe flats. As the sun breaks through the trees on the edge of the plains, the buffalo are already moving. This daily routine creates

Elephant on the Chobe River flood plains have a mudbath to protect their sensitive skin.

a spectacular sight as the sun filters through the dust they kick up. Even companions usually reluctant to rise this early thank me after seeing this spectacle and are duly impressed by my bushcraft savvy. I am reluctant to tell them that this happens every morning, and everyone knows it.

Serondella is only a few miles from Kasane, a small town on the northern border of Botswana. This is where

Namibia, Zambia, Zimbabwe and Botswana meet. Victoria Falls in Zimbabwe is within easy reach of Kasane and the Chobe park and this has become a well-travelled route.

Botswana continues to be the destination of choice for those who want a real African experience and are prepared to work for it.

Hundreds of buffalo gather as their path to water is disturbed by vehicles on the dusty park roads.

*Buffalo on the Chobe River
at dawn*

Extracts from the notebooks above:
...The baboons are still a menace but so enjoyable to watch...

A group of travellers, obviously new to this area, pitched their camp and went off for a game-viewing drive. Their camp which proudly displayed their provisions was immediately raided by baboons, monkeys and banded mongoose...

During the night I watched a porcupine inspect our camp. The quills make quite a noise as they rustle when they move.

Gabar goshawk (Micronisus gabar)

Lions of Namibia

ON MY FIRST VISIT I WAS captivated by Namibia. It was 1977 and I had just embarked on a new career as a full-time painter, knowing full well through bad experiences that a painter of wildlife has to know not only his animals and their anatomy but also their habitat.

NAMIBIA

If I was going to paint the animals of Namibia, I had to get to know the country. South West Africa, as Namibia was called, was a long tiring drive from my home on the east coast of South Africa. To complicate matters, the speed limit was about 45 mph, petrol sales were restricted to daytime purchases only, and carrying fuel in cans was prohibited. My old Volkswagen van had a pathetic fuel range and required a lot of coaxing just to make it to the next town. The towns are few and far between in South Africa's Karoo and in Namibia.

eros

9 months

24 months

30 months

Kudu montage

Red-billed Quelea. Described by ROBERTS: BIRDS OF SOUTH AFRICA as "a superabundant species...... truly comparable with locusts."

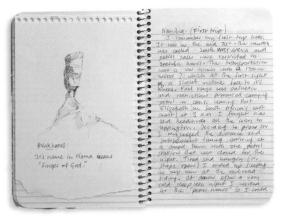

Brinkaros
It's name in Nama means "Singel of God."

This snail's pace had its positive side as I had plenty of time to take in the countryside and enjoy the wild, rugged land. It is a peculiar feature of dry, monochromatic places that they become so colourful in the late afternoon and early morning light. Namibia is like a chameleon. As the sinking sunrays caress the landscape, nature becomes the watercolourist, laying subtle washes of colour that gently change hue as they mingle and are tinted by a reddening sun. An even more conspicuous and equally enjoyable aspect of travelling here is the lack of traffic. Namibia has a very sparse population and one is more likely to encounter a wild animal than another traveller on some roads. As one who gravitates to wide open places crowded with animals rather than people, I found that this was the place for me, and my

many visits since that first trip underscore this. Namibia is a special place that has a unique landscape, a wilderness habitat that borders on the bizarre, with an unusual mix of people.

German influences abound in the architecture although they are somewhat out of place in a dry, desert land. This scene is further surprising when a group of Herero women appear in their colourful full-length Victorian-era dresses: missionaries promoted this fashion for the sake of modesty. Namibia's rich tapestry of native people includes the Wambo, Kavango, Herero, Damara, Nama and the San (Bushmen), all small but distinctive groups of rich heritage. It is precisely this mixture of unusual people, displaced architecture, and barren landscape that is so appealing and unique.

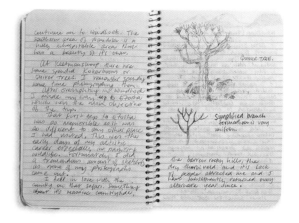

QUIVER TREE.

Simplified branch formation is very uniform.

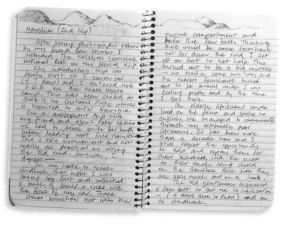

Extracts from the notebooks above:
...I remember my first trip here. It was in the mid-70s. The country was called South West Africa and petrol sales were restricted to specific hours... I fought hills and headwinds all the way to Uppington ... I misjudged the distance and the subsequent timing, arriving at a small town with one petrol station that was closed for the night ... I ended up sleeping in my van...

(2nd trip) ...In my haste to reach Windhoek that night I was driving too fast ... stones somehow got into the engine and broke the fan belt... I set off on foot to get help. This turned out to be big mistake – no traffic came my way and the nearest farmhouse turned out to be several miles. I was feeling pretty bad by the time I got there.

Oryx and a flock of guinea fowl share a waterhole at dusk.

In broad terms, Namibia is divided into three distinct regions. A central escarpment and plateau run like a spine from the northern to the southern end of the country. This central zone is bordered by the Kalahari desert to the east and the Namib coastal desert to the west.

Namibia has little rainfall, and it is notoriously unreliable. The country is desperately short of surface water, relying on natural springs, artesian wells and man-made dams and boreholes.

The main road to the north follows the central plateau leading mainly through terrain wooded with acacia and combretum trees and bushes; this is where rainfall is highest. My usual desire to get out of cities even applies in Africa, in this case meaning Windhoek,

the largest centre in the country. Namibia has only recently negotiated its way out of both colonial and minority rule but Windhoek's roads are still dominated by the favoured sedan of the former rulers, the Mercedes Benz.

I take the road north which leads to Etosha and the Caprivi strip, a long sliver of land that stretches eastward, all the way to where the Chobe and Zambezi rivers meet. The small town of Okahandja an hour or so out of Windhoek is a good stop for stocking up on safari provisions, which must include biltong, a local dried meat product that is a delicacy in southern Africa. Biltong is an acquired taste that also requires a broken-in stomach, as my son Matthew found out the hard way on a trip he shared with me in 1996. The popularity of biltong and

venison has in a way improved not only game populations but attitudes towards wildlife. Game ranching – raising wild animals for commercial purposes – has developed enormously and the old attitude of treating as vermin any creature that competed with domestic stock has faded. This change in attitude has resulted in a dramatic increase in the numbers of herbivores on privately owned properties.

Another change in attitudes among ranchers involves the endangered cheetah, but this only came about through many years of dogged work by a remarkable woman. Laurie Marker, who founded the Cheetah Conservation Fund in 1990, is solely responsible for educating Namibians on this fragile predator. Research by Laurie and her staff has given her the ammunition

Wildebeest

Cheetah are commonly known as the fastest animals on earth and to see them at full speed is breathtaking.

Cheetah (Acinonyx jubatus)

required to show the ranchers that destroying cheetah on their farms had an opposite effect to that intended. The ecological gaps created by shooting them soon attracted more cheetah to fill the unclaimed range.

CCF has introduced an unusual method of protecting livestock. Anatolian Shepherd dogs are raised with the livestock, which they adopt as family, and the presence of these large dogs is enough to deter the cheetah.

Thanks to the generous help from many supporters, including Phil Osborne of Atlanta and Carl Hilker, the CCF cheetah sanctuary in Namibia totals 40,000 acres. This sanctuary is at the core of a larger conservancy created through cooperation with neighbouring ranches and sits at the foothills of Waterberg Plateau Park. CCF is a growing concern, both in research, educational and conservation programmes and in its facilities to accommodate visitors.

It brings me great joy to visit Laurie, to see the progress and the success CCF is enjoying. It is encouraging to see an endangered species being given new hope, and it is refreshing to see how people who care can make a difference. It is important to get involved and support a body such as the Cheetah Conservation Fund. This and similar organizations rely on the private sector for donations, as university and government grants are spread thin with many needy causes. The trick is to support an outfit like CCF, where your money is spent in the field.

Cheetah patrol their territory in search of food.

Extracts from the notebooks on the right:
Cheetah Conservation Fund.

Chewbaaka, Laurie's tame cheetah has changed since I last saw him. He is now in his prime and has an almost arrogant attitude and seldom blesses you with direct eye contact.

CCF have 8 cheetah on the ranch. They are here on a temporary basis waiting for relocation. We are able to be with them at feeding time and our presence makes them extremely nervous.

Oddly enough although the cheetah is much in demand as they are very rare and have genetic problems which make their future unstable, they are very difficult to place. Etosha National Park for example has little or no cheetah left because of anthrax but the Namibian Parks Board do not want to replace them.

ETOSHA —
"Place of dry water"

springbuck ♂
(horns are slender)

Red hartebeest
(alcelaphus buselaphus)

Note long, oversized head.
has dark (almost black) markings
on all four legs and the front of
it's face. It is a rather awkward-
looking animal.

July 31ˢᵗ 1996 — Kalkheuwel waterho
(West of Ft. Namutoni) — Game coun
58 Giraffe — 9 bull ele
37 eland — 76 kudu
43 gemsbuck — 44 black
± 310 zebra — ±235 sprin
8 kori bustards — 2 ost
— 18 warthe

Etosha montage

Bat-eared foxes

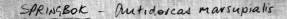

SPRINGBOK - Antidorcas marsupialis

PRONK - From the Afrikaans word: "to show off".
(mainly a juvenile and sub-adult behaviour)
more frequent immediately after rain)

used as an orientation

white dorsal crest -
dorsal gland saturated the long white & dark hair on the back. This scent is released during pronking.

drawing proportion to illustrate "norm".

Both sexes have horns.
(♂ heavier)

Restricted to Namibia, the Kalahari & the Karoo.

The Springbok has a long haired white dorsal crest from the middle of the back to the rump.
This long white hair is normally seen only when it is erected during pronking.

PRONKING is associated when the animal is excited or alarmed.

Head lowered, back arched feet together. - Also breaks into an exagerated step / trot.

Stuart / Kingdon.

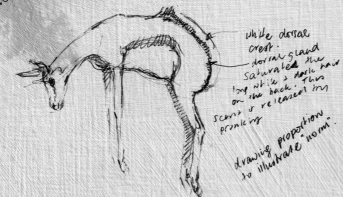

Springbuck (Antidorcas marsupialis)
Herero: Menyeh ~ Tswana: Tshephe ~ Nama/Damara: Gûb. ~ Afrikaans: Springbok.

Both sexes have short horns.

The Springbuck has a long white dorsal crest from the middle of the back to the buttocks.
This long white hair is normally seen only when it is erected during pronking.

Springbuck montage

ETOSHA NATIONAL PARK

Etosha National Park dominates the pages of this chapter in much the same way the park has occupied most of my time in Namibia. This is not to lessen the value or importance of other wilderness areas but rather illustrates my love of Etosha.

I have travelled to this park in northern Namibia on so many occasions that I have lost count (perhaps nine times?). There has been a lot of private development on its southern border that feeds off the Etosha. The camps have grown with the increase in tourism, but the park itself seems to be timeless. Today Fort Namutoni is one of the three camps inside the park borders. On my first visit, the only accommodation other than camping was within the fort. The original rooms varied in size based on military rank. Mine must have housed someone who ranked lower than private, as it was only slightly larger than a bed and had a narrow 'gun-slit' as a window. The oppressive heat outside was greatly increased inside by the lack of air circulation.

At 1,800 square miles, Etosha Pan is vast. Animals are drawn to the natural fountains that surface along its southern perimeter as the pan seldom has surface water. The pan is a remnant of an even larger ancient lake, now just a memory like

George Cuvier: Anatomie Comparée, Paris 1849

those at Nxai and Makgadikgadi in Botswana. The park takes its name from this pan: Etosha means 'great white place', 'place of dry water' or 'place of mirages'.

All three descriptions are apt. Mirages dance across the flat white surface. This image has played an important role in my artistic endeavours and I have attempted to capture it for the last 22 years.

Etosha wilderness area today is much reduced compared to the vast terrain once available to wildlife, but has an increased animal population which requires sensitive and expert management for its protection. Two outstanding men in this field come to mind and I hope that I honour them by this mention. They are the former chief research biologist Dr Hu Berry and park veterinarian Dr Ian Hofmeyr, who lost his

Gemsbuck

Royal pose

life early. The Etosha is the result of hard work and constant readjustment to ensure a balance between terrain and inhabitants now that the major long-distance migrations of yesteryear can take place no more. In some cases, enthusiasm has unexpected effects and the researchers have had to rethink their strategy. This was the case with the introduction of nearly fifty artificial watering points, intended to spread the animals and reduce seasonal migration. The programme was possibly too successful: animals started to destroy the vegetation around waterholes by their constant presence and growing numbers. This forced the closure of many waterholes to get the small-scale migration back in operation. Anthrax is another of Etosha's real concerns and overuse of watering points by the animals compounded the problem.

It is easy to understand how some people would not find Etosha attractive. It is a hot, dry, dusty place and the sun bounds off the white ground in a blazingly bright light that etches into your brain. It is a desolate, barren expanse in the middle of nowhere, at times reluctant to share its treasures. But artists are drawn to Etosha, as the open places and the animals' need to frequent the waterholes makes for excellent game viewing. The quality of light, although not a photographer's choice, is especially interesting late in the day and a different palette is required to render faithfully the subtle yellows, pinks and tinted greys. It is these nuances that delight an artist's eye and make Etosha come alive.

There is a 'changing of the guard' within the National Parks of Namibia as the new government employs more native inhabitants to replace the former predominantly Afrikaans staff. This is a sensitive issue. What is important to me is not who does the job but that it is done well. It is my wish that the National Parks continue to receive the funds they require to maintain what already exists and that research and conservation will continue to be a priority.

This painting was given the title Talking Back. *These zebra put on an extremely noisy performance for reasons unknown which reminded me of a typical human teenager-parent confrontation.*

A herd of wildebeest make their daily trek to the fountains on the edge of the Etosha Pan.

Kudu portraiture

Extracts from the notebooks on the left:
Animals repeat certain positions which with patience allows you to sketch a characteristic behaviour and get the anatomy right.

It is July – the middle of the dry winter season and the Okaukuejo area is exceptionally dry. All the waterholes have a steady stream of thirsty animals visiting.

to make our way to Halali Camp in the middle of the park. I have travelled to Etosha many times. My last trip in 1996 was with my son Matthew. This is a similar safari at the same time of the year with my friend Les Allison and his son Clay. It is a real pleasure for me to introduce them to Etosha and Namibia. This is a unique country which is very different from the rest of Africa.

Today on our return to Ft. Namutoni we came upon a lone mature lion who was walking in a determined manner in

Extract from the notebook above:
I have travelled to Etosha many times. This is a similar safari… with my friend Les Allison and his son, Clay. It is a real pleasure for me to introduce them to Etosha and Namibia. This is a unique country which is very different from the rest of Africa.

Ostrich at Okondeka Fountain in the dry western side of the Pan

Field study, Etosha Pan waterhole

Extract from the notebooks on the right:
Bat-eared foxes can be seen by observant, patient visitors. It is hard to believe but we have not seen any damara dik-dik... Maybe we'll have some luck tomorrow.

Extracts from the notebooks on the left:
Etosha's elephant look almost white which is
a result of 'dusting' with the white soil found
in the park. At sundown, the red sun can
make the elephant look pink.

Impala in flight

For most of the year, except during the short rainy season, Etosha is a 'waterhole park'. Wildlife is reliant on the few watering points. Despite the danger of predators, animals must make daily treks to quench their thirst. These points can become pretty crowded with an interesting mix of animals and birds. It requires patience to get the full benefit of game viewing at a waterhole, as habits and preferences vary among species. One day, my son and I spent much of the day at a waterhole and were rewarded by seeing a leopard make an unsuccessful attempt at killing a young zebra. This happened right in front of us, no more than a few yards away. Afterwards I thought of the people who had just left and felt sorry for them. Game viewing is like a vignette of all our lives. It can be uneventful some of the time but the harder you work at it, the more you get out of it.

Zebra study the terrain for predators as they cautiously approach waterholes.

Traffic at the waterholes increases in the late morning hours as several species drink at the same time.

THE NAMIB

If the bizarre or the unusual is your preference, then the Namib should top your list of places to visit. This desert derives its unusual climatic conditions from a cold ocean current that chills the air, producing a great bank of condensation. The fog that rolls inshore covers the dunes in a fine layer of life-giving moisture. The Skeleton Coast to the north has earned its name. Skeletons of shipwrecks bear testament to the unforgiving nature of this remote coastline.

The Namib-Naukluft Park is one of the largest in the world. It offers tranquility and solitude for those seeking it, and it is a place where the only people you are likely to see are those travelling in your party. Sandwich Harbour was once a deepwater port used by early fishermen, but there is little evidence left. The desert has a way of reclaiming its territory. Today Sandwich plays host to a wide variety of birds including pelicans and lesser flamingoes. Access, by permit only, requires a lowtide drive along the beach from Walvis Bay. Walvis Bay is also an important stopover for wetland birds and the huge flocks that gather along the coast make for fine viewing.

Massive dunes provide a graphic backdrop to flamingoes as they take to the air.

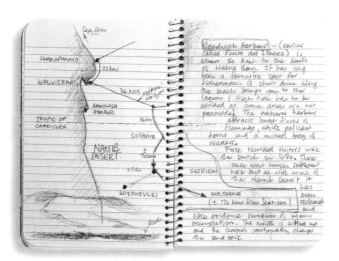

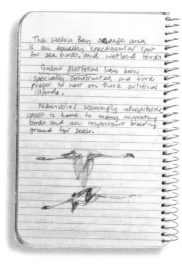

Extracts from the notebooks on the left:
Sandwich Harbour. The natural harbour attracts huge flocks of flamingo, white pelicans, terns and a mixed bag of waders.

The Walvis Bay sewage area is an equally spectacular spot for seabirds and wetland birds. Guano platforms have been specially constructed and birds prefer to nest on these artificial islands.

Namibia's seemingly inhospitable coast is home to many migrating birds and an important breeding ground for seals.

Sossusvlei

Red hues due to iron oxide in the sand.
Colours and shapes change rapidly with the rise & fall
of the sun.

The Sossusvlei dunes are the
highest shifting sand dunes in
the world.

*The notebooks on the left
and below read:*
*Sossusvlei. Red hues due to
iron oxide in the sand.
Colours and shapes change
rapidly with the rise and fall
of the sun. The Sossusvlei
dunes are the highest
shifting sand dunes in the
world. Abstract in nature –
ever changing – always
the same.*

ABSTRACT IN NATURE ~ EVER CHANGING ~ ALWAYS THE SAME

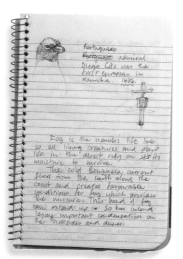

Extracts from the notebooks on the left and right:
Portuguese Admiral Diego Cao was the first European in Namibia 1486.
*Fog is the Namib's lifeline as all living creatures and plant life in the desert rely on its
moisture to survive... This band of fog can extend up to 50 km inland...*

*The road to Sesriem and Sossusvlei goes through a diverse landscape from gravel open
plains to rocky hills and dunes.*

*It is remarkable how a monochromatic landscape becomes so vibrant with colours
that change hues by the minute as the sun lowers. Hues vary from whites to oranges
to red ochre and some spectacular maroon shades.*

A camel-thorn tree is dwarfed by the enormous dune in the background.

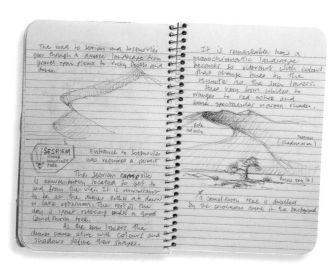

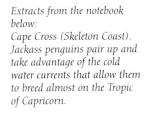

SOSSUSVLEI

Sossusvlei, deep in the red heart of the Namib, is a magnet for photographers, amateur and professional alike. For self-proclaimed creative individuals, this place is a lesson in graphic art and design on a scale that leaves you breathless. The dunes at Sossus are colossal, some of the highest in the world. They are continually changing as the wind chisels away at the forms like a sculptor and the casting shadows glide across the slopes and contours. During the heat of the day we lie motionless while the dunes shimmer, a well-selected tree providing shade for a siesta as we wait for better photographic opportunities with the sinking of the sun.

North of Walvis Bay at Cape Cross is a sanctuary for many thousands of Cape fur seals. If one is looking for solitude and a quiet spot, this is not the place. The din and the stench are overwhelming. I have not yet visited the immense wilderness in the northern sector of Namibia called Kaokoland, the home of the Himba tribe and the Kaokoland elephant. But it's on my list!

Field journal

Lizard buzzard

Field Journal - Sept. 1993.
Lake McIlwaine

Monkey Orange-tree
(Strychnos spinosa.)

STEENBOK (steinbuck)
Raphicerus campestris.

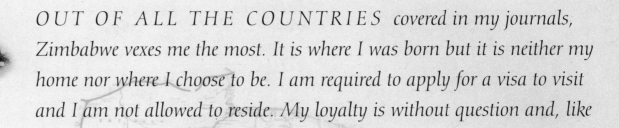

OUT OF ALL THE COUNTRIES covered in my journals, Zimbabwe vexes me the most. It is where I was born but it is neither my home nor where I choose to be. I am required to apply for a visa to visit and I am not allowed to reside. My loyalty is without question and, like

ZIMBABWE

most of my fellows who are living outside the country, I make the annual journey 'back home'.

Zimbabwe invited me to explore its raw beauty and by my mid-teens I had done solo trips all over the countryside. Looking back on this period I am amazed not only at my independence but also at the fact that my parents allowed it. Several members of my family had an appreciation for the arts, which influenced me at an early age, and my love for the arts and the bushveld grew simultaneously. My early days were spent on the family farm with a bunch of mostly older cousins. Our preoccupations were hunting, fishing and exploring along with the sons of the farm labourers. These friends of ours were of the Mashona tribe and spoke no English, so the only way to communicate was through the use of a hybrid language called Fanakalo.

Zimbabwe falls within the tropics, although apart from the slender strips of lowveld, the elevation above sea level is fairly high, giving it a moderate climate and mild temperatures. This made for an outdoor lifestyle, and as much of the country is rural or wilderness, nosing around in the bush was both cheap and easily arranged.

THE LAND BETWEEN THE LIMPOPO AND THE ZAMBEZI........

"THE PEACEFULNESS OF IT ALL; THE CHAOTIC GRANDEUR. IT
CREATES A FEELING OF AWE AND BRINGS HOME TO US HOW
VERY SMALL WE ARE."   CECIL JOHN RHODES

THE MATOPO HILLS.
now called
MATOBO.
'The Hills' is an
appropriate name – Huge
smooth whaleback hills &
smaller granite boulders
that appear stacked to
make up "CASTLE KOPJES"
dominate the area. This
area falls under National
Parks &
also the
National
museums.

A VIEW OF THE WORLD

Cecil John Rhodes.
Allan Wilson and his
party, Leander Starr
Jameson and Charles
Patrick John Coghlan
are all buried here.

"The Painted Hills"
Matopos is home to stone
age art, estimated between
1500 to 10 000 years ago. Most
produced between 8000 years
ago with some art even older.

Zimbabwe montage

Right: Raptor montage

Extract from the notebook on the left:
The Matopo Hills. Now called Matobo. 'The Hills' is an appropriate name – huge, smooth whaleback hills and smaller granite boulders that appear stacked to make up 'castle kopjes' dominate the area.

A View of the World. Cecil John Rhodes, Allan Wilson and his party, Leander Starr Jameson and Charles Patrick John Coghlan are all buried here.

Extract from the notebook on the left:
The Painted Hills. Matopos is home to stone age art estimated between 1,500 to 10,000 years ago. Most produced between 8,000 and 10,000 years ago with some art even older.

This country has witnessed many changes. Early occupants were the San (Bushmen) who gloried their world in paintings on cave walls and granite koppies. These gentle people were replaced by ancestors of today's Shona tribes, who created the Great Zimbabwe culture. Their flourishing empire is evident today in the form of the Great Zimbabwe Ruins. The Ndebele, an offshoot of the Zulu tribe in South Africa, then took up residence in the south-west and built themselves into a mighty force. Some 50 years later they were followed by the 'Pioneer Column' of white settlers. The occupation of the country was the obsession of Cecil J. Rhodes, whose vision and accomplishment command respect even if you disapprove of his imperialist intentions. He was given the honorary warrior salute by the Ndebele elders at his burial in the Matopos, which indicates the respect he earned

Ndebele warriors in ceremonial battle dress

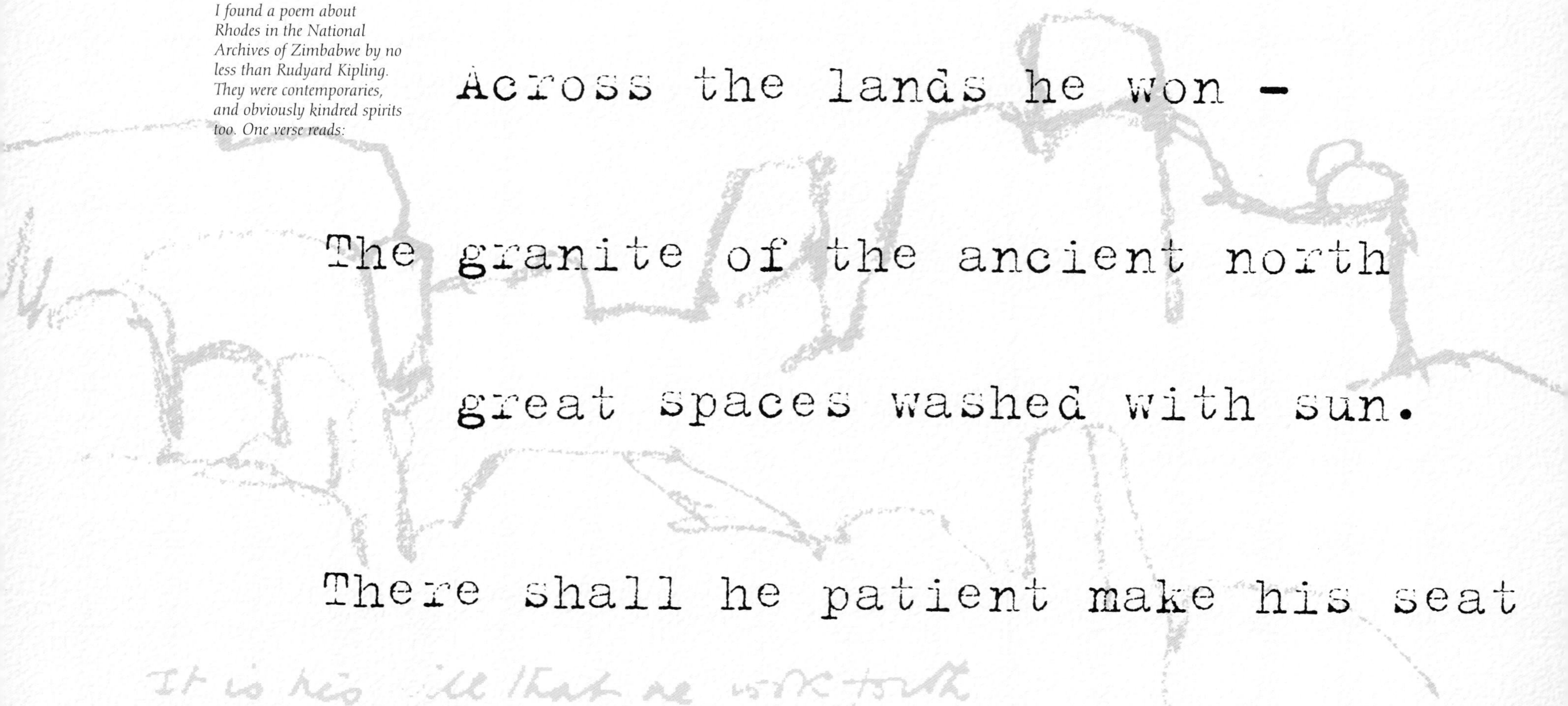

It is his will that he look forth

I found a poem about Rhodes in the National Archives of Zimbabwe by no less than Rudyard Kipling. They were contemporaries, and obviously kindred spirits too. One verse reads:

Across the lands he won —

The granite of the ancient north

great spaces washed with sun.

There shall he patient make his seat

(as when the death he dared)

And there await a people's feet

In the paths that he prepared.

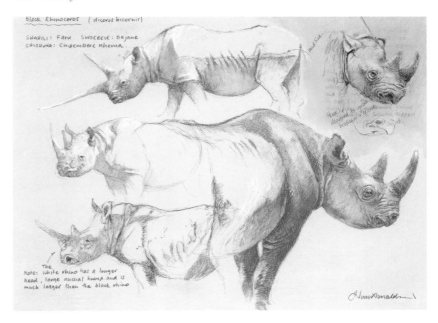

Rhino montage

even from those he vanquished. The Matobo Hills National Park, as it is now called, is small by African standards but not in importance. Not only is it a unique wilderness area but it is also home to historic sights that include the grave of C. J. Rhodes. The Matopos also hosted a significant period in the country's history when the defiant Ndebele fought against the northward advance of colonial occupation. Spectacular hills and bare granite koppies dominate the landscape. Matobo means 'bald heads'. Massive rocks lunge out of the ground. These in turn have more rocks piled high on top of them, giving them the local names of balancing rocks and castle koppies. The rocky hills are a haven for many birds of prey, notably the black eagle. Its prime food of choice, the hyrax, is in abundant supply. These rare birds are renowned for their acrobatic displays, which include a free-fall tumble as they grasp each other by the claws and fall out of the sky.

The park has splendid rhino populations and armed guards are employed to protect them. White rhino are numerous enough to allow relocating some to other areas. The black rhino is also surviving in the Matopos. The signature of this place is probably the artwork of the San people who were so in tune with their environment. Even today the spiritual significance it had in their lives is communicated to us through their art. Much of the art is abstract in design with a stylized quality. The paintings are primarily symbolic and more difficult to explain than if they were narrative in nature. They underscore the mystique of the Matobo and stand as a reminder that we are here for a very short period in time and it is our responsibility to respect and conserve these natural wonders.

Hyrax montage

HWANGE NATIONAL PARK

Hwange National Park is the largest designated wildlife area in Zimbabwe and is home to the greatest variety of animals and bird species. Hwange benefits from a buffer provided by state and privately owned lands that share with it an interest in conservation. This benefit is clearly illustrated by the success of conservation efforts within the Hwange Estate, which borders Hwange National Park. Alan Elliot's book, *The Presidential Elephants of Zimbabwe* chronicles this turn of events that benefitted the greater geographical area.

Much of Hwange falls within the Kalahari sands. Calcrete deposits containing a variety of compounds that the sands lack attract a constant flow of animals and make for excellent game viewing areas. A calcrete pan near the park gate by the main camp entrance has

Zimbabwe montage 2

Old jumbo cow

JULY 1997 - HWANGE, ZIMBABWE

WINTERS ARE MY FAVOURITE TIME IN THE BUSHVELD.
THE COLD WINTER NIGHTS AND EARLY MORNING
FROSTS "DRY OUT" THE VEGETATION, LEAVING A
WASHED-OUT AUTUMN LOOK. THE THICK GREEN
BUSH THAT MAKES GAME VIEWING AND BIRD
WATCHING SO DIFFICULT IS LONG GONE AND THE
COOL AIR IS DRY AND CLEAR.
NOW THAT I LIVE FAR AWAY, THIS IS THE TIME
I MISS AFRICA THE MOST.

Sable antelope

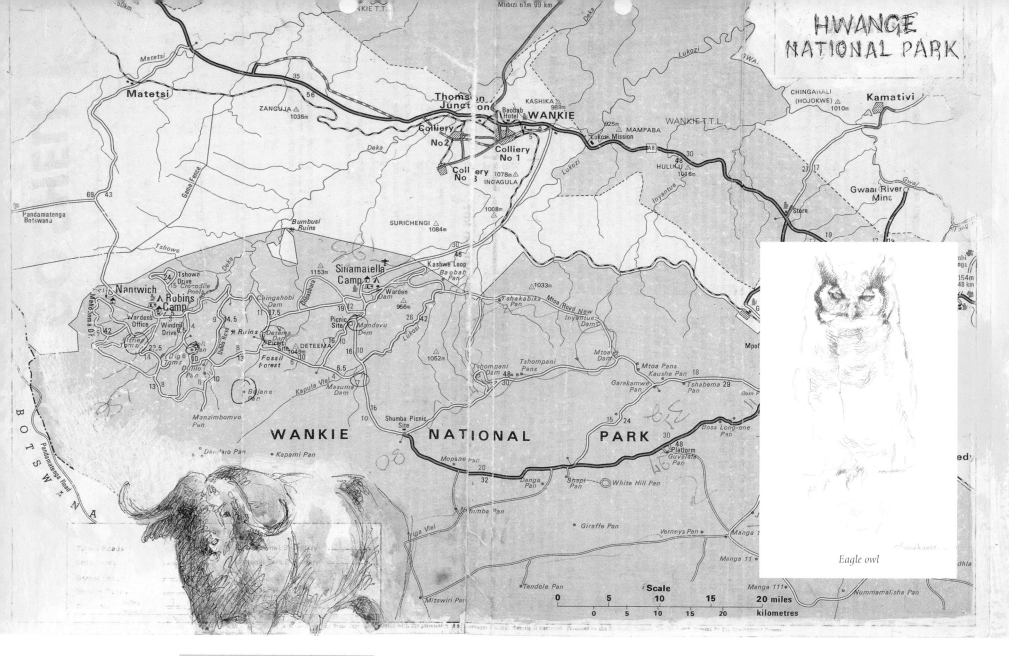

Eagle owl

*Sable
portraiture*

always been a good viewing spot for this reason. 'Black cotton' soils are also found in the park, particularly in the north-east. These soils make driving difficult in the rainy season and are best avoided, even with a four-wheel-drive vehicle.

The winter months of May to August are the dry season, when there is a tremendous temperature variation between day and night due to a rapid heat loss by thermal radiation. Frost is common in the lower lying vleis and this 'knocks back' the vegetation.

Seasons are not sharply defined in the African bushveld. Transitions are dictated by the rains more than temperatures. The change from summer to autumn is subdued, but leaves do change colour and fall from the trees and bushes. The spring is preceded by the extreme heat of October as all the remaining moisture is sucked from the parched land. October is known as suicide month; life seems to come to a standstill as all energy is sapped. Clouds build up in the afternoons and the promise of rain has everyone looking up in hope.

New life explodes as if in celebration after the first rains. Within two days the barren ground is covered in greenery and flowers spring out of nowhere; pans fill and frogs appear everywhere.

Hwange has been at the forefront of controversy with its game management policy of culling elephants and other animals. Elephant pressure can quickly cause major and long term loss of vegetation. Apart from protecting the vegetation, the argument for culling is that local people benefit from the meat and that the funds derived from the controlled sales of ivory and skin are ploughed back into the system, thereby protecting the elephant and the park itself.

The argument against culling is that elephants respond to a whole range of factors and will naturally reduce their population following a reduction in their food supply. Culling, which reduces their numbers unnaturally, therefore has the opposite effect; they counter the human intervention of culling by stepping up their rate of reproduction.

Hwange is home to Zimbabwe's largest elephant populations, as it once was for rhino. Sadly, the black rhino has been poached out of the park in the last decade, even though their numbers were bolstered by 40 additional animals in the mid-1960s. Large herds of buffalo are spread thoughout the park. The magnificent sable and the tawny roan antelope have stable populations and are regularly seen, especially as they nervously approach the waterholes for their daily drink.

THE PRESIDENTIAL HERD

Over the past 20 years, Alan Elliot and his guides have built up a unique association with a herd of elephants that are descendants of harassed and persecuted crop-raiding outcasts. These

Alan Elliot and friend

Zebra cross an open area in the Mopane woodlands, Hwange.

Leopard studies

elephant, now protected by a presidential decree, number some 300 and accept the close presence of vehicles and their occupants. This special relationship illustrates the elephants' capacity to accept non-threatening humans and provides an opportunity for scientists and conservationists to study wild African elephants up close and in their natural environment. I have travelled to Hwange on several occasions since the early 1970s. As well as having cousins Kerry and Mike Fynn working there for the national parks, I was based at Hwange during my short and undistinguished military career. Military operations involved short (one-day) and longer (three-day) patrols, which gave us the opportunity to stroll around the bushveld and enjoy the area immediately surrounding the Hwange park. Animals both large and small were encountered daily and produced different degrees of adrenaline depending on the circumstances.

These patrols gave us some wonderful experiences. Every soldier I meet from those days talks not about the bad times but rather about the close encounters with the wild animals and the sometimes hilarious reactions of fellow soldiers. As soldiers, we were instructed not to shoot any animals even in self-defence, and this proved particularly hazardous with some black rhino, which have an unfortunate habit of charging for no perceptible reason. It was fairly common for a patrol to have to climb trees hurriedly to avoid the angry attention of a rhino.

SEPTEMBER 1993 — HWANGE, ZIMBABWE.

TODAY'S EVENTS WERE RATHER UNUSUAL. BEAT, MY DRIVER & GUIDE, AND I HAD BEEN DRIVING AROUND FOR MOST OF THE DAY WITHOUT SEEING MUCH WHEN WE CAME ACROSS A LEOPARD. PERCHED TOO HIGH IN THE TREE FOR ITS OWN GOOD, THE LEOPARD WAS EXTREMELY AGITATED. WE SOON FOUND OUT THE REASON FOR HIS PREDICAMENT — A LION WAS HARASSING HIM AND, WHILST THIS WAS HAPPENING, DOZENS OF VULTURES HAD DESCENDED ON HIS IMPALA KILL, WHICH WAS STASHED IN ANOTHER TREE 50 YARDS AWAY.

THERE WAS NOTHING THE LEOPARD COULD DO TO SAVE HIS DINNER WHILE THE LION WAS AROUND. THE VULTURES KNOCKED THE CARCASS OUT OF THE TREE DURING THE FEEDING FRENZY, WHICH DISTRACTED THE LION'S ATTENTION FROM THE LEOPARD. AS IF WE WERE PART OF THE PECKING ORDER, WHEN THE LEOPARD CAME DOWN — SOMEWHAT UNGRACEFULLY — HE VENTED HIS ANGER AT US IN A BRIEF BUT FRIGHTENING CHARGE BEFORE DISAPPEARING INTO THE THICK BUSH BY THE RIVER'S EDGE.

A large tusker moves through the dry Mopane in Hwange.

Test of strength

Extract from notes on the pioneering work of Ted Davison:

In 1928, at the age of 22, Ted Davison arrived by himself at Wankie to establish a national park. With an annual budget of £500 his first task was to explore and map the 5,000 square miles of 'Wankie National Park'. In his travels to also educate and inform local people of the new rules he earned the name Dumbanyika – 'the one who travels through the wilderness'.

Victoria Falls

'Scenes so lovely must have been
gazed upon by angels in their flight.'

David Livingstone

VICTORIA FALLS

The scale is massive... The sound rumbles and crashes like thunder and makes the very earth tremble... It is a spectacle of overwhelming godly power. The only other natural place to make me feel I was in an area created by some greater being is the Ngorongoro Crater in Tanzania. *Mosi oa tunya* – 'the smoke that thunders' – however is more than spectacular. It is a place of homage and reflection and puts one's worldly significance in perspective.

I have to wonder what David Livingstone would think of Victoria Falls today. It has become one of the most commercial tourist hot spots in the whole of Africa. How would he react to a 'faux African' hotel in the middle of Africa – to the bungee-jumpers, river-rafters and microlight-flyers who need more than Victoria Falls and an African wilderness safari to keep them stimulated? But if the village has gone very commercial, fortunately the falls themselves remain one of the true wonders of the world. Here the Zambezi River is *a mile* (1,600 m) wide and plunges 354 feet (108 m). Devil's Cataract on the extreme western side is the lowest fall and subsequently carries the most water. The main falls are the next lowest area and carry a substantial volume of water even during the dry season. The dry season is the best time to see the falls as there is too much spray when the river is high. Zambezi National Park to the north of the falls has a substantial number of elephant but it is most noted for its sable antelope. Victoria Falls National Park south of the falls borders the gorge. Thomas Baines spent 12 days sketching the falls from every possible angle in 1861. His paintings were the first recorded images to portray the grandeur and beauty of these waters to the world.

Photographs on these two pages are courtesy of the National Archives of Zimbabwe.

African tribal dancers entertain visitors.

Elephant bulls, Zambezi Valley

THE ZAMBEZI VALLEY

The Zambezi Valley, or as it is locally known, the Valley, is demarcated by an escarpment on both the Zambian and Zimbabwean sides. Every time I journey to the Valley, I like to stop at the top of the escarpment to spend a little time taking in the wonderful vista below. This is Africa at its raw, untamed best – this is what the first adventurers saw and glorified in their journals. It feels like home, and I am in awe. Dust devils mark the thermals as they dance their way across the flat plains below. Baobab trees, which are known to reach more than 3,000 years old, stand tall and proud above the jessebush, symbolic of the lowveld. This is 'Big Five' country and where the adventure begins.

Zimbabweans are spellbound by the Zambezi Valley, paying homage to it in the number of books written on it. *The Zambezi: River of the Gods* by Jan and

The Zambezi Valley. The Zambezi is the fourth largest river system in Africa.

Buffalo montage

Fiona Teede; *Spirit of the Zambezi* by Jeff and Veronica Stutchbury; *Zambezi: River of Africa* by Mike Coppinger and Jumbo Williams and Michael Maik's *Zambezi: Journey of a River* are all magnificent works that I proudly display in my library. The Zambezi is the fourth largest river system in Africa. Its unique value lies in its being light on human settlement and having extensive areas along the banks under state protected parks or controlled hunting concession areas. The controversial tsetse plays an important role in limiting human occupation of the Valley and attempts to eradicate the fly are condemned by all conservationists without exception. Canoe safaris have become popular on the river. Not only are they an environmentally perfect use, but canoes offer an ideally quiet, unobtrusive way of seeing wildlife along the river. Tourism has increased on the river since the government allowed private individuals and companies to operate camps and canoe and walking safaris.

The Zambezi breaks into channels as it meanders through the Valley, forming islands that are frequented by elephant, buffalo and waterbuck. The prevailing wind blows upstream, providing a little relief from the usually hot conditions. This is a peaceful place to be, where the number of visitors is suitably restricted and camps are well-spaced to provide a secluded environment.

MATUSADONA NATIONAL PARK

In 1959 Kariba dam wall was completed, creating one of the world's largest man-made lakes and the current shoreline for the Matusadona park. The local residents, the Tonga people, were moved to higher ground against their wishes. They believed that it was impossible to dam the mighty Zambezi River and that the River God, Nyaminyami, would not allow it to happen.

As the waters rose, filling the lower valley, animals were stranded on shrinking islands and had to swim to higher ground or drown. Rupert Fothergill led a team of national park employees on a harrowing rescue code named Operation Noah. Their heroic efforts over several gruelling years saved many thousands of animals from certain death. Dead trees stand high like proud monuments to the dead and have become a Kariba landmark. Cape buffalo frequent the water's edge, where periodically receding waters have created open grassland. Matusadona is best seen from a boat to appreciate the variety of birds and animals along the shoreline. The splendid African fish eagle makes use of the dead trees at the water's edge as perches to look for fish and as ideal nesting sites to raise its young.

In 1982 I did an extensive safari over a four-month period, which included travel to South Africa, Namibia, Botswana and Zimbabwe. After spending a week in the Gonarezhou I headed for the Zambezi Valley. Matusadona is accessible by road, then warden, John Stevens. Too embarrased to tell him of my predicament, after dark I went back to the camp area, selected a suitable tree to sleep under, and did the best I could. Fortunately it was a warm night and I managed to get some sleep but I woke up feeling pretty awful. Some old friends of mine, Sue and Frik Maas, arrived from Fothergill Island, which pleased me greatly, but I continued to feel poorly. After I spent another uncomfortable night under my 'favourite tree', Frik arranged for a boat to take me back to Kariba township. I finally saw a doctor back in South Africa. After feeling ill with a high fever for much of my four-month safari and losing an awful lot of weight, I was diagnosed with tickbite fever. One tablet had me feeling better very quickly and I remember being angry with myself for not seeking help sooner.

Buffalo, Matusadona National Park

Nyaminyami photograph courtesy of the National Archives of Zimbabwe

but as my old truck was somewhat unreliable I chose to hire a boat to take me directly from Kariba township. This was my first trip to the park and I was totally unprepared, having brought nothing with me except a few changes of clothing and my sketching equipment. The park had a designated campsite and an ablution block – that was it. I was the only person in the camp apart from a young English woman who was responsible for the campsite. I went up to the park HQ to introduce myself to the

Spoonbills, home to roost, Lake Kariba

Sunset over Kariba

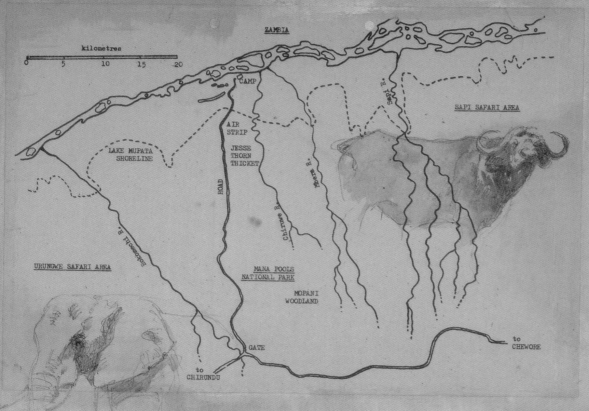

Rhino studies

MANA POOLS NATIONAL PARK

Mana Pools National Park has a unique quality in today's Africa. Animals are free to walk into camp and people are free to walk in the wild. Over the years this has resulted in human/animal confrontations where the former have come off second best. It is however this arrangement that makes Mana Pools so special. The Zambezi, marking the park's northern border, is at its spectacular best at this point in its long journey to the Indian Ocean. Along the banks of the Zambezi are four large pools which give the area its name.

During the dry months (May to October), the animals are forced to come to the waterholes and the river from deep within the dry areas along the escarpment. Although there is little grass left at this season (termites being the biggest consumers) Natal mahogany, Acacia albida and sausage trees provide food and shade.

Originally these pools relied on the annual flooding of the Zambezi to fill them, but since the construction of Kariba's wall, the floods are controlled by man and not by nature. The pools now depend on the rains to fill them.

Termites have increased alarmingly since the annual flooding of the aptly named Zambezi flood plain has been stopped, and they are having a long term effect on the area. Another phenomenon that seems to be occuring at Mana Pools is that the large trees are dying out, and there is little indication of a new generation coming up to replace them. Possibly this also is a result of changes in the surface waters since the dam impounded the Zambezi, or it may reflect termite impact, or browsing animals compromising tree recruitment.

Above: Zebra and mahogany, Mana Pools   *Below: Young zebra*

I have had the privilege of visiting Mana Pools and the surrounding areas many times over the past two decades. My cousin Stretch Ferriera, who owns Goliath Safaris and operates in this part of the Valley, has always been very generous in assisting me in my ongoing quest for reference material. Stretch often takes a busman's holiday and joins me in the Valley. He has on occasion taken advantage of the situation to use me as a guinea pig to try out new walking safari routes and seems to derive a lot of pleasure from my discomfort.

I was fortunate to visit here in the mid-1970s when black rhino could be seen on a daily basis. Today there are no more. All that is left is a graveyard of hundreds of skulls at the park's HQ compound – a powerful illustration of human greed and its consequences.

My son Matthew and our tent share some Mana real estate with an elephant bull.

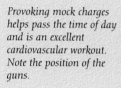

Provoking mock charges helps pass the time of day and is an excellent cardiovascular workout. Note the position of the guns.

Stretch Ferreira and Willie de Beer fool around beneath a confused jumbo.

Willie de Beer and I bunked in this tent and campsite on the banks of the Zambezi. He believes that if the tent is left open at night, the wind blows the mosquitos out.

Baobab tree

A waterbuck and a troop of baboons share the upper reaches of Long Pool.

Unwanted guests at breakfast.

Grooming is an important social interaction.

Sentry.

Chacma baboon (papio ursinus)

Termite mounds as tall as elephant!

"The pajama look"

Midday in the Chewore. Elephant bulls seek the shade of the baobab tree.

Serval

OCTOBER 1972 — LOWER ZAMBEZI VALLEY.

WE ARE RESTING NOW. EVEN THOUGH IT IS ONLY 10:30 AM. OUR PATROL 'STICK' IS WORN OUT FROM THE BRUTAL HEAT, WHICH SAPS ONE'S ENERGY AND MAKES IT IMPOSSIBLE TO QUENCH YOUR THIRST. BITING TSETSE FLIES AND THE IRRITATING MOPANE FLY ADD TO OUR DISCOMFORT. THEY ARE MORE ABUNDANT HERE AT THE FOOT OF THE ESCARPMENT THAN THEY WERE CLOSER TO THE RIVER. DISCOMFORTS ASIDE, I FEEL A TRUE SENSE OF BELONGING — THIS IS THE GREAT AFRICAN ADVENTURE — THE LAND OF THE GIANTS, OF BAOBABS AND ELEPHANTS AND WE ARE PRIVILEGED TO BE HERE.

Today we are rewarded with a wonderful interaction with a couple of elephant as we canoe down the Zambezi River. Reacting to our steady downstream travel, these young bulls chose to cross the channel directly in front of us. Disturbed by our unavoidable close presence these bulls felt threatened and hurried to climb the right-hand bank.

In their haste, they started 'fighting' amongst themselves with the two older bulls pushing the youngest back and blocking his escape route. He in turn picked on us as we became part of the pecking order.

Zambezi River, Mana Pools, Zimbabwe

River crossing

GONAREZHOU

Gonarezhou is a rugged and remote stretch of lowveld in the south-eastern corner of the country. Its name, meaning 'the place of elephants', is appropriate as this is indeed elephant country. After years of war and poaching, the local elephant have rightly earned a reputation of being highly strung and prone to aggression. Several years ago my cousin Mike Fynn, who was then the warden of the Mabalauta area, and I were enjoying some peaceful moments at the Mafukus pan when he suddenly took off in great haste for his truck. Somewhat confused, I followed his lead. In an instant we were half surrounded by a large milling herd of elephant. These were

not the vehicle- and human-tolerant elephant of most parks but touchy and extremely dangerous animals. We hastily retreated a few hundred yards and watched the herd nervously drink, still conscious of our presence.

The Gonarezhou is fed by two rivers, the Runde in the north and the Mwenezi in the extreme south. This spectacular wilderness has a checkered past, having had a particularly active military presence during the civil wars. Minefields laid by the defence forces continued to cause casualties, especially amongst the elephant, which do not recognize international borders. The Chipinda pools and the red-stone Chilojo cliffs are other landmarks of the park. The more remote

and less visited Mabalauta in the south sustains a profusion of big game and is more familiar to me because of my family association. There are no internal roads connecting the northern area and the south and the vast wilderness in between remains relatively untravelled.

Gonarezhou's big game populations, like those in many other remote areas in Africa, have suffered from poaching. Large tracts of land are not accessible by road. This, coupled with limited conservation funds and manpower has given the poachers the upper hand. That dreaded African curse, drought, hit Gonarezhou a

Buffalo bulls: a tribute to one of my favourite contemporary painters, Oleg Stravrowsky

KIM DONALDSON

To Rutenga & Chiredzi

Park Boundary

Luwungwa

Luwungwa Drive

Mtoma Dr.

Nyamugwe Pan (W)

Twiza Siding

Mtoma Pan (W)

Ntabamnomvu Drive

RED HILLS

Nyala Siding

Nyala Rd

NUANETSI

MABALAUTA NAT. PARKS H.Q

Swimuwini Rest Camp

1

2

BUFFALO BEND

Machisani

Mwatombo Loop

Lipakwa Pan (W)

Manyanda Pan (W)

Sotshangana Dr.

Lipakwa Dr

3

TI SAFARI EA

Makonde Loop

Mafukus Pan (W)

4

Chibewe Loop

MALAPATI PARKS H.Q.

MALIPATI STORE

MANJINJI PAN Bird Sanctuary

NUANETSI

Old Mana lion

Nuanetsi River

MARCH 1982 - GONAREZHOU

AS THE SUN LOWERS IN THE WEST, THE SHADOWS LENGTHEN
ACROSS THE SANDY RIVERBED OF THE NUANETSI RIVER. A
LONE NYALA EWE CROSSES THE OPENING TO DRINK AT THE
CHANNEL ON THE FAR SIDE. EVER NERVOUS, SHE REACTS
TO THE NEARBY CLATTER OF A FLOCK OF GUINEAFOWL AS
THEY MAKE THEIR WAY HOME TO ROOST. TWO ELEPHANTS
APPEAR OUT OF NOWHERE, LIKE SILENT GIANTS. THEY GLIDE
ACROSS THE RIVERBED, HALTING IN UNISON AS THEY CATCH
MY SCENT. THEY PAUSE, RAISE THEIR TRUNKS AND TRY TO
LOCATE THE INTRUDER. BY STAYING PERFECTLY STILL,
I KEEP THEM FROM SEEING ME, AND IN A FEW MINUTES,
DISAPPEAR WITHOUT A SOUND.
THE NIGHT IS CLOSING IN AND I HEAD BACK TO THE PARK
H.Q. BEFORE IT IS COMPLETELY DARK.

few years back and had a devastating effect on local people and wildlife. Thousands of starving animals were fed by farmers and volunteers. Many animals were captured and translocated to better areas.

This is not the first time Gonarezhou's animals have been under such extreme pressure. Foot-and-mouth disease outbreaks that are deadly for domestic cattle have qualified the area as a 'redzone' and all buffalo herds in the vicinity have been exterminated.

But Africa is a land of feast or famine, of good and bad times, and has a history of reviving and rejuvenating itself. With good management and a little luck with the weather, nature will take care of itself. In recent times Clem Coetzee, a man with an almost supernatural reputation in game capture and animal translocation, did the unheard of. His team relocated 200 elephant, including adults, out of the overpopulated park.

There are some positive reports on the area. Exceptionally good rains have fallen and the new warden is being praised for his commitment to the future of Gonarezhou.

Zimbabwe as a whole remains vexing. Will government be able to restore sufficient calm to keep tourists coming for the long future? Wild places need little infrastructure, and in fact profit from having so little in the way of roads and development.

Ironically, periods of political upheaval can help to keep wild places wild. My love for all things wild was born in Zimbabwe and I wish the country and all its people and wildlife fortitude.

Jumbo bull study

Buffalo, disturbed by human presence, delay their w

FEW PLACES OR EVENTS have created in me such a high state of anticipation as my first visit to Kenya. For years, my nationality and the political punishment for my place of birth prevented me from travelling to many African countries, including Kenya. This is the showcase of Africa and I wanted to experience it. I would never have the audacity to call myself a student of African history as I have a memory like a sieve, but I'm attracted to the writings and stories of the other adventurers. Kenya has been a magnet for some interesting people and has been celebrated by the likes

KENYA

of Karen Blixen, Ernest Hemingway, Robert Ruark, George and Joy Adamson and many great photographers. Kenya saw the best and the worst of the colonial era, always with its wildlife and wildlands and richly varied tribal heritage in the spotlight. Big game hunting closed here in 1977, and since then game-viewing safaris have flourished increasingly. For most people in Europe and North America, Kenya epitomizes Africa.

My first trip commenced with landing at Nairobi, the capital, which has the same old look of most Third World cities. Although there were a few places I needed to visit in collecting information for this book, I was eager to get out into the country and leave seeing Nairobi for a later date. As I was not familiar with getting around, I hired a driver and vehicle for the duration of my safari. He was an old hand at this, having taken countless clients before me, but my requirements were rather specialized as I had come to work and not to play. We immediately started butting heads and I grew dubious about the whole venture. Having grown up in Africa and having spent a lot of time in the wild, I was used to having my life placed in danger, but in Kenya, that danger is from the drivers, including mine. Some fierce negotiation produced an arrangement that required compromises from both parties, and the safari turned out to be very successful.

Lion cubs study

Starlings, unlike oxpeckers, do not feed on animal parasites. They use the zebra as a platform and feed on insects that are disturbed by their host.

My first challenge was in adjusting to the presence of a new species in this home of the African safari: the tourist minivan. (Yes, I was in one myself, although the only eager head besides the driver's in my van was my own.) I have had the luxury and freedom of staying in places where I could camp and walk wherever I chose, and it cost me some effort to adapt to the hordes of minivans that roar around at breakneck speeds in their haste to visit all the 'required' spots. My driver was instructed to depart from the normal routine of gravitating to where these vans collected, which of course meant there was something interesting to see. Instead, we would go off on our own. It is not that I have anything against these people; ironically, like my fellow artists and photographers, I probably have some part in attracting people to come on safari. It is just that I need quieter circumstances to be able to take in the images fully. The wildlife doesn't seem to mind about the visitors, and the animals' approachability certainly has advantages. Numerous companies specialize in providing more exclusive types of guided and walking safaris, if that is one's preference. Good planning is the key and after you have become familiar with the country, more adventurous self-drive trips are the way to go. The roads in Kenya are badly potholed and speedbumps are sometimes placed across the road with no warning signs, which can lead to accidents. At one point on the main road to the north from Nairobi, a three-foot-deep ditch had been dug across the entire road. There was no warning and the cars that wrecked were piled high on the side of the road. The dust on some of these cars suggested that they had been there for several weeks and that the fiasco was ongoing. When driving in Kenya, the word 'caution' takes on a new meaning.

This somewhat strange sight of a cow in the back of a truck with nothing but a rope over its back becomes less bizarre after one spends more time on Kenya's roads.

Barn owl
(Tyto alba)

The notebook on the left reads:
Northern Frontier District. Kenya – nearly half of Kenya is semi-desert. Most of this low rainfall area is in the north and was commonly known as the Northern Frontier District or NFD.

The NFD is inhabited by five main tribes – Turkana, Rendille and Samburu, Gabbra and Boran. This area is home for the beisa oryx, reticulated giraffe, Grevy's zebra, gerenuk. Both the Guenther's and Kirk's dik-dik also inhabit parts of this region.

Samburu maidens

Extracts from the notebook below:
Exotic plants – bougainvillaea, frangipani, etc. enhance the rich riverine vegetation. Monkeys and a monitor lizard move through the camp and ignore me completely.

Buffalo Springs, as the name suggests, was famous for its huge herds of buffalo. However the population was decimated by a prolonged drought in 1978 when the river completely dried up.

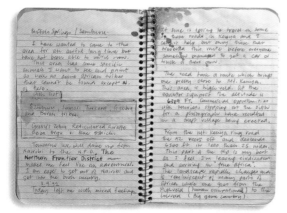

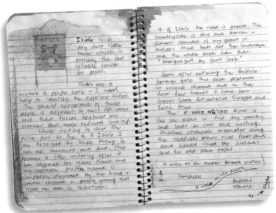

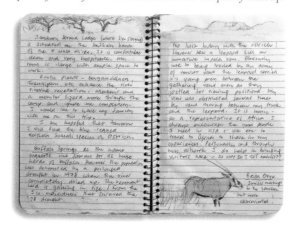

Extract from the notebook above:
Buffalo Springs/Samburu. This area has some specific animals I want to see and paint as well as some African tribes that cannot be found except N. of here.

The road took a route which brings one pretty close to Mt Kenya. This area is high-veld. At the equator signpost the altitude is 6,389 ft.

Extract from the notebook above:
Isiolo is a dry dust little town which is possibly the last reliable source for petrol.

North of Isiolo the road is gravel. The countryside is dry and barren – almost denuded of any grass or bushes. Mud huts dot the landscape and the whole area has that 'overgrazed by goat' look.

Samburu landscape

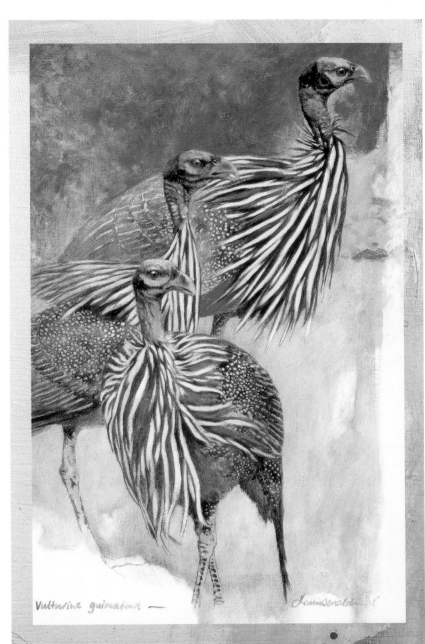

Vulturine guineafowl —

KIM DONALDSON.

VULTURINE GUINEA FOWL

Several species of fowl inhabit Africa but none is as brilliantly coloured as the vulturine guinea fowl. A band of chestnut downy feathers cover the otherwise bald head and long spearhead-shaped feathers in black and white drape over those of iridescent blue. Its bright red eyes complete the palette, contrasting sharply with the arid landscape.

SAMBURU

In the Northern Territory lives an interesting tribe at least as distinctive as the Maasai: the Samburu. Like the Maasai they have a great love for cattle and their search for grazing and water categorizes them as semi-nomadic pastoralists. They also keep goats, sheep, donkeys and camels but it is cattle that constitute their wealth.

The Samburu do not cultivate the land, believing it belongs to everyone. This is probably a good philosophy as the Northern Frontier District in which they live is a hot, dry, inhospitable expanse with very little water.

The Samburu have powerful moral and social codes which ensure their collective well-being and protect their customs and rituals. For generations they have retained a pride in their identity, living in precarious harmony with a harsh land that forces them to be mobile. This ability to live with seeming ease and dignity in such a difficult place intrigues the Western mind. I forget who wrote that out in the wilderness one loses the need to make an impact, but it is certainly true of the Samburu. They do not find it necessary to change their ways to impress others. I found the Samburu to have an aloof manner much like that of the cat that seldom grants us a direct look. Thomasin Magor wrote a splendid book on the Samburu called *African Warriors* that is loaded with superb photographs and represents this proud tribe with the respect they deserve. I envy and applaud her for the time she spent with the Samburu.

Samburu youth

Two young Samburu warriors stand in unity and in competition as they gaze upon the available women in their tribe.

KAREN BLIXEN

Karen Blixen (who wrote under the name Isak Dinesen) is probably the most celebrated of the writers who have focused on Kenya, and for good reason, as she was such a fine writer. Adventures are one thing, but description that captures the force of things African upon the European mind is quite another. Few authors from the different world of several decades ago speak to us with such sharply evocative insight.

I thought of her acquaintance with people of various tribes as I made my own brief acquaintance with the Samburu. Speaking of the Kikuyu, she wrote: 'I have met the eyes of my native companions and have felt that we were at a great distance from one another... Perhaps they were, in life itself, within their own element, such as we can never be.'

The power of her life and her stories – even when mass-marketed in a feature film, but especially when read in the originals – is that they still convey essentials of Africa that are not easy to express. She saw that her embodiment of Africa was her own great work. 'I was up at a great height upon the roof of the world – I did not know that I was at the height and upon the roof of my own life.' (*Isak Dinesen*, Peter Beard 1963:45)

SAMBURU-BUFFALO SPRINGS

Samburu-Buffalo Springs up in the dry northern Samburu country is two separate parks that are run by two individual local councils. They share the Ewaso Nyiro River as a joint boundary and lifeline. The Ewaso Nyiro, which in the Maa language of the Samburu means 'river of brown water' is not brown but crystal clear and extremely inviting in its hot, dry surroundings. I can only assume that the name derives from the reddish-brown, flat riverbed. This river also passes through the Shaba National Reserve (where Joy Adamson worked and met her untimely death) before disappearing into the Lorian swamp. The river with its tall doum palms and riverine vegetation is the central focus of the parks. The huge granite mountain, Lololokwe, stands tall in the north, providing a spectacular backdrop and contrast to the herds of reddish-coloured elephant.

This is the area that George Adamson writes about in his book *My Pride and Joy*. He was posted here as the first game warden and based at the little town of Isiolo to the south. His budget was non-existent and he relied on camels and donkeys for transportation and to patrol the enormous wilderness placed under his care. He writes that despite efforts to protect them, the elephants in Kenya today are only 20 per cent of their previous numbers and that the black rhino has fared even worse.

George Adamson wrote about his brother Terence's belief that there is a brotherhood between man and elephant. To illustrate this bond, Terence told George about an elephant that had become trapped in a well. His road-building gang wanted the animal killed for meat but Terence chose to try and free it. By dropping stones into the well, the floor was slowly raised. The elephant calmly lifted its feet as the men filled the well, understanding exactly what was happening. 'Terence had kept murmuring reassurance to the elephant throughout its ordeal and occasionally patted its anxious and questioning trunk. Once free the elephant moved slowly towards him as if in thanks; it was some time before Terence could persuade it to return to its herd.'

This area is called Buffalo Springs as it was home to large buffalo herds. In 1978 a severe drought killed off all but a dozen buffalo as the Ewaso Nyiro river dried up. Today the buffalo have increased, but like the elephant, which have been heavily poached, they are a shadow of their former populations.

The Buffalo Springs and Samburu wilderness is a pleasant surprise as it is a lovely area with beautiful river acacia trees and some mountain ranges that provide a little relief from an otherwise flat landscape. This is an excellent location to see some of Africa's rare animals. These include the reticulated giraffe, Grevy's zebra, beisa oryx, gerenuk and the tiny dik-dik. The ostrich found here is the blue-legged Somali subspecies and this area is also home to the vulturine guinea fowl.

Some of these animals and birds are not unique to this region but there is no question that this is the place to see all of them. The reticulated giraffe is such a rich colour that it seems almost out of place. Its striking pattern makes its cousins in southern Africa look thoroughly plain. Had I been exposed to this animal years ago, I would have painted many more giraffes. The Grevy's zebra is another

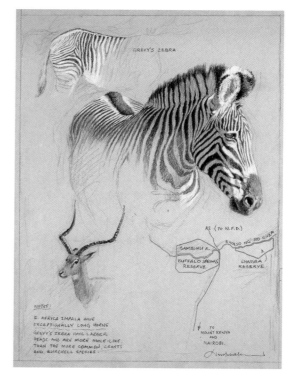

'most beautiful' subspecies within its family. It has an exceedingly large head and gives an impression of mild curiosity. These zebra can easily be seen in small groups of several animals, unlike the more common Burchell's zebra, which lives in larger herds.

If the local giraffe and zebra are the most handsome of their kind, the gerenuk has to be the most unfortunate antelope. Equipped with an excessively long neck, the gerenuk has evolved to be able to dine on bushes and low trees that competing browsers cannot reach. The design may be efficient but I find the gerenuk's appearance on the bizarre side and I felt no inclination to draw one.

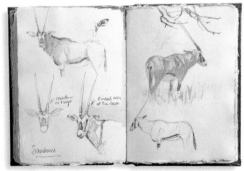

The notebook on the left reads:
Gerenuk have an 'unfortunate' look about them and are not very attractive. The gerenuk have a habit of feeding off bushes opposite to where you look at them, making it more difficult to see them well.

Samburu's impala have spectacular horns and are much longer than those found in southern Africa.

Keeping low to the ground and using cover the bush provides, a leopard stalks its prey.

Enough roads cross these parks for the animals to be tolerant of vehicles, so that one gets good game viewing from up close. Here I came face to face with the great trade-off in game viewing: if you visit places where vehicles are a rarity or animals are hunted, the game tends to be cautious and skittish about your approach, but where animals are habituated to vehicles and expect no harm, you tend to run across other vehicles and not have the wildlife to yourself. I had a special moment at Samburu-Buffalo Springs that illustrates this contradiction. My driver had found a leopard on the prowl. Finding a leopard

hunting in the daylight is unusual in itself, and we followed as it stalked an animal that was hidden from our view. The leopard lunged in liquid action and disappeared from our sight in a cloud of dust. Moments later it reappeared carrying a young gazelle in its mouth. My elation at witnessing this soon yielded to a shameful intolerance of other vehicles on my part, however, even though the leopard seemed utterly unfazed about our presence. As several minivans jostled for position, I lost my temper at their intrusion and entered into a fruitless screaming match with one of the drivers. I'm embarrassed at my response in the heat of the moment, answering one discourtesy with another. The leopard, I suppose, never cared one way or other. (It walked between the vans with its kill, climbed a tree and set about dinner.)

These parks are run by the Samburu people and do not have the controls of the more disciplined Kenya Wildlife Services. Some drivers abuse the freedom of being able to leave the roads, which does the habitat no favours. One hopes these tribal-run parks will hold their own in the network of Kenya's conservation areas. I look forward to another trip to the Northern Frontier soon which I hope will include more time to sketch the Samburu and other interesting tribes of the region.

A young Samburu warrior performs a traditional dance. These dancers delight in attaining a great height with these leaps. Good technique appears to be important and feet must be kept together. The dance is closely observed by the other men while the young ladies, who the performance is for, pretend to be uninterested.

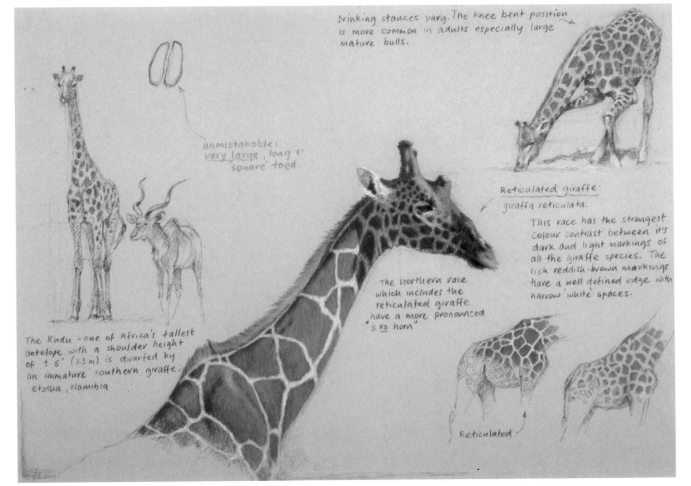

Drinking stances vary. The knee bent position is more common in adults especially large mature bulls.

unmistakable: very large, long & 'square' toed.

Reticulated giraffe: giraffa reticulata.

This race has the strongest colour contrast between it's dark and light markings of all the giraffe species. The rich reddish-brown markings have a well defined edge with narrow white spaces.

The Northern race which includes the reticulated giraffe. have a more pronounced "3 RD horn"

The Kudu - one of Africa's tallest antelope with a shoulder height of ± 5' (1.5m) is dwarfed by an immature southern giraffe. Etosha, Namibia

Reticulated

Giraffe montage

YOU, WHO ARE NIGHT & DAY IN ONE BODY — YOU, WHO ARE DARK & LIGHT IN ONE FORM — YOU, WHO ARE GOOD & EVIL IN ONE SHAPE — ANIMAL OF TWO COLOURS, ANIMAL OF PERFECT HARMONY........

Grevy's zebra

MAASAI MARA

The Maasai Mara is the most celebrated of all the reserves in Kenya. Together, and part of the same ecosystem, the Serengeti in Tanzania and the Mara in Kenya make up the most renowned wildlife mecca in Africa. The Mara-Serengeti deserves this reputation as it is a wonderland that attracts massive herds of animals the like of which can be seen nowhere else. The Kenyan extension of the Serengeti plains in the Mara is home to the northern reaches of the famous wildebeest migration which follows the rains and the need for better grazing. The migration, in addition to approximately 1.5 million wildebeest, includes an estimated 500,000 gazelles and 250,000 zebra. As noted in the Tanzania chapter, this is in part a modern phenomenon affected by veterinary medicine controlling some diseases that formerly kept animal numbers down. The increased populations have enforced a wider migrational circle.

In their quest for seasonal grazing, the great herds formerly did not reach as far as the Mara and stayed within the Serengeti and south of the Kenyan border. Dr Bernhard Grzimek's research in the Serengeti provides interesting reading as it included comprehensive game counts and annual migration estimates. Although his records targeted the Serengeti they give an overall picture of the ecosystem fifty years ago and illustrate the changes that have affected the Mara.

In addition to the immense concentration of animals, the

A territorial wildebeest waiting out a passing storm.

Mara has over 450 species of birds, including 53 kinds of birds of prey. In general, the best area for game viewing is the Mara Triangle, situated in the less arid western section. Even though the Mara is not a large park by African standards, only a small area of it is visited by tourists. The Maasai occupy the bulk of the reserve for grazing their cattle.

A spotted hyaena claims his share of a muddy kill.

Cheetah (acinonyx jubatus)
Ndebele: Ihlosi ~ Shangaan: Khankankha ~ Swahili: Duma ~ Nama/Damara: Arub ~ Chishona: Dindingwa ~ Ovambo: Shinga.

Immature ♂ - Central Serengeti
October '97

Cheetah are holding their own in the Maasai Mara, an open savannah that is ideal for them to use their speed and run down prey.

Lion study

Wildebeest arrive in the Mara with the rains.

This park is good for seeing animals all year round. Predators do not migrate with the herds and the open terrain provides unhindered viewing. The Mara will remain a major drawcard for safari travellers, especially those who want to share in the wonder but have a limited time available.

Two young cheetah nearing adulthood
share a warthog kill with their mother.

Cheetah in full flight

BURCHELL'S ZEBRA
Equus (Hippotigris) burchelli

Typical knee biting/kneeling posture in both playful and real fighting.

Bachelor stallions group together on the perimeter of breeding herds. These stallions engage in playful fighting. Attack and defense skills are required if an animal is to accrue & maintain his own herd.

Biting the opponents knees is the target of choice which is countered by kneeling.

The ears (forward facing) illustrate that these animals are in a non-aggressive mood and that their behaviour is playful. In full-scale fights the stallions will have their ears back in an aggressive posture.

Amboseli (Kenya) variation has a shorter mane especially between the ears at the top of the head.

Zebra fighting

AMBOSELI

Amboseli is a startlingly photogenic place because of its position: Kilimanjaro Mountain is the most spectacular backdrop to this gathering place for animals. As an artist I am enthralled by the place's contrasting beauty: I am completely mesmerized. It is hard to say what the focal point is in Amboseli. Kilimanjaro dominates the horizon and is the most photographed and painted image in Africa. No one could ignore its presence. The swamps could be the epicentre as this is where the animals concentrate. Much of Amboseli is dry and barren with numerous dead trees scattered about. The winds that blow in a westerly direction kick up the dust and dust devils continually move across the land. It is an easy place to study animals up close, which is an obvious advantage to someone sketching them. I find the way to do this is to drive around and find a suitable setting or group of animals. There I make myself comfortable, allow the animals or birds I want to sketch and

Old Maasai woman

photograph time to get used to my being around, and then I spend most of the day working in that spot. It is this 'still period' that allows the wildlife time to settle so that animals begin to behave as if I were not there at all.

Sketching moving animals requires repetition as it is difficult to capture anatomy faithfully in a fleeting moment. Animals have postures and characteristics that they repeat, and recording these needs the patience to wait for the right moments.

I get some curious looks from other people as I sit out in the noonday sun doing my work. Conversation is discouraged by my ignoring their presence. This is a little unfriendly, but it's more or less a case of the place being 'my office' and I don't like to be disturbed. The act of painting has for me always been a private endeavour, one that doesn't lend itself to sociable exchange.

Zebra fighting

An elephant bull with spectacular tusks takes a pause beneath a fever tree.

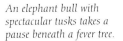

Extracts from the notebooks below:
Amboseli, Kenya. a.m. drive from Nairobi –
south to Namanga. Tar road all the way is
pretty good but deep potholes are a problem.
Other drivers, however, present a real danger.
Masai huts are low to the ground and
surrounded by thorn bushes.

From Namanga the road to Amboseli is dirt
and very corrugated. (It is no better than the
last time I was here.) Masai villages dot the
countryside and young boys herding cattle go
about their business. After completing the
endless paperwork at the park gate we cross
Lake Amboseli heading directly for Ol-tukai.

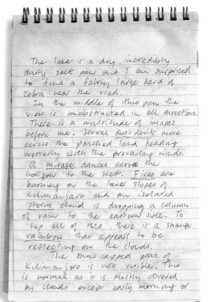

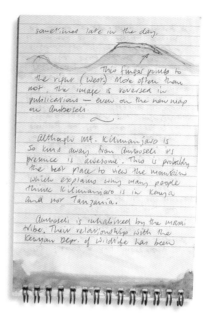

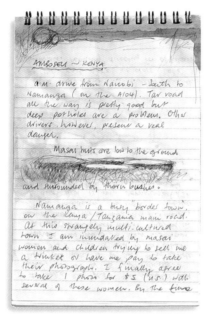

Extracts from the notebooks above and below:
The lake is a dry, incredibly dusty salt-pan
and I am surprised to find a fairly large herd
of zebra near the road.

A mirage dances across the horizon to the
west. Fires are burning on the lower slopes of
Kilimanjaro and an isolated storm cloud is
dropping a column of rain to the eastern side.
Although Mt Kilimanjaro is 50 kms away

from Amboseli, its presence is awesome.
This is probably the best place to view the
mountain which explains why many people
think Kilimanjaro is in Kenya and not in
Tanzania.

Even though it is not what it once was, I just
love Amboseli. It truly is a magical place and
remains one of my favourite places to visit.

Black rhino (Diceros bicornis)

KIM DONALDSON

An elephant breeding herd moves through the heat haze as a dust devil dances across the foothills of Kilimanjaro.

My timing in visiting Amboseli was not ideal. The black rhino that the park was famous for had all but been wiped out. I have never seen any here and I could not find out if any were left. Supposedly the Maasai, who lived here before the area was declared protected, retaliated against certain restrictions by killing the rhino, or perhaps more commercial impulses were operating. Either way, Amboseli's precious rhino were reduced from about 150 in 1950 to eight in 1977. Not only did this 'get back' at the Kenyan authorities as the Maasai knew the rhino were a key element in the park's appeal, but it also was in keeping with their belief that spearing a dangerous animal confirmed one's bravery. The rhino is considered second only to the lion as a challenge.

Two famous rhinos, a mother and daughter called Gertie and Gladys, noted for long, thin, almost horizontal horns, are no more. With them an image has died and the world is the poorer for this.

The large, mature fever trees and acacias are also fighting for

Lion study

Zebra mother and foal

survival, only their enemy comes from beneath in the form of increased salinity. It is a sad sight to see much of the landscape dotted with fallen trees. Broken trunks and branches are now a feature of the land and characteristic images of Amboseli.

Kenya was the first great African wildlife show and it retains its lofty position as an animal showcase. It has a slightly tarnished image among wilderness purists, but this is inevitable because of its popularity and the economic opportunity its natural wonders provide. As the wildlife becomes restricted by human populations, and natural movements of game are confined to demarcated zones, management has to step up. Conservation is everyone's concern but policies need to benefit people if they are to succeed.

So did Kenya measure up to my eager anticipation? It did without question. To a southern African eye the very open vistas are pretty much unlike anything further south, where the savannah is mostly more wooded or much drier. You cannot get the same sense of plenty where you can only see a few yards or a few hundred yards. When one has anticipated something for a long time and built up expectations, one is open to disappointment. Kenya did not disappoint me. As an artist, I am eager to get back for another safari. As a conservationist, I rejoiced in the volume of animals and birdlife. The healthy numbers of cheetah were especially rewarding to see as they have become rare in other places.

AMBOSELI, KENYA

As Zebra weave their way along ancient trails between grazing and water, Kilimanjaro rises high and proud in the background.

The "cool" looking mountain with its permanent snow cap is a sharp contrast to the hot, dry landscape of Amboseli

Map of East Africa, date unknown,
attributed to Rowland Ward Limited,
London (in Neumann 1898:449)

A young kudu interrupts its drinking to check for predators.

TANZANIA IS THE SETTING of the Serengeti Plain and the famous Mount Kilimanjaro, archaeological treasures, rich cultural diversity, and millions of animals.

Kilimanjaro, Ngorongoro Crater and the Serengeti are undoubtedly the main attractions, but there are several other wilderness areas worth visiting. These parks, such as the Selous and Ruaha in the south, are largely undeveloped and more difficult to reach.

TANZANIA

Bananas in Tanzania come in a variety of colours but taste the same.

The Tarangire National Park falls in between the heavily visited north and the less travelled south. It is easily accessible from Arusha but is less well-known and has fewer visitors than the Ngorongoro Conservation Area and the Serengeti. Since I have not been to the Ruaha wilderness area and my short visit to Selous National Park was spoilt by unseasonal rains, I have not covered them in this chapter.

Tanzania has the distinction that nearly one quarter of its area has been set aside for parks or reserves and Ngorongoro, Serengeti and Selous have been declared World Heritage Sites by UNESCO.

Lion and cub

<u>Maasai</u> - Lion hunting was a popular test of bravery and the bravest Morani (warriors) were awarded the lion's mane headdress (olawaru) after a successful hunt. Fortunately for lions, the Maasai are no longer allowed to hunt them. The enkuraru (ostrich feather headdress) was worn in battle as it gave an illusion of great height and subsequently a psychological advantage over the enemy.

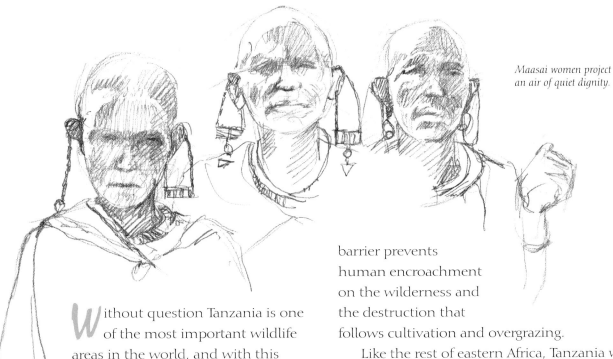

*Maasai women project
an air of quiet dignity.*

Without question Tanzania is one of the most important wildlife areas in the world, and with this natural resource comes the responsibility to protect and conserve it. This country has had less European intrusion than many other African countries, and this has probably had a positive effect on the wilderness and its wildlife. Tanzania's wild lands never saw the decimation of wildlife that European settlers brought about in southern Africa or parts of North Africa.

The big game was extensively hunted by white hunters, but this was mostly limited to the more easily accessible areas to the north and the coastal belt.

Bernhard Grzimek and his son Michael conducted the first game survey in Tanzania, which eventually led to the Serengeti being enlarged to its present size. Dr Grzimek quickly realized the important role the tsetse fly played in conservation. In his enlightening book *Serengeti Shall Not Die*, Dr Grzimek writes that the tsetse fly is the only 'true friend' the elephants and zebras have, for it makes their homeland uninhabitable for people. Domestic animals, the most precious possessions of many African tribes, do not have the immunity to the fly that the indigenous wild animals have. This natural barrier prevents human encroachment on the wilderness and the destruction that follows cultivation and overgrazing.

Like the rest of eastern Africa, Tanzania was formed by massive earth upheavals creating the Rift Valley and the highest and lowest points on the African continent. The Rift Valley is clearly defined by the lakes, steep valley walls and mountains. This is where the big game can be found, along with the famous Maasai people. The Maasai dominated the other tribes with their warlike traditions. However, they lived in harmony with the land and the wildlife, relying on their domestic animals for food and protecting the countryside from overgrazing by practising a nomadic existence. Zebra and wildebeest herds lived alongside the Maasai cattle. With the arrival of Europeans came the desire to own land and set boundaries. With settlers came modern medicine, which soon had an impact on the populations of humans and domestic herds. Germany took the country by force but surrendered control to Britain under the Treaty of Versailles following the First World War. Tanganyika, as the British renamed it, was to be governed as a Trust Territory in the interests of the native inhabitants. One positive action brought about by British rule was the ending of slavery in 1922. Tanzania received its independence from Britain in 1961, with Zanzibar and Pemba being included in 1963.

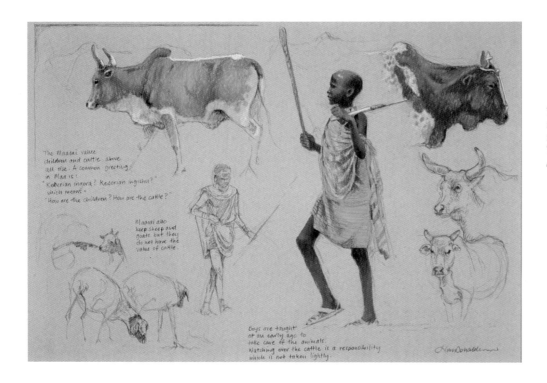

The Maasai value children and cattle above all else. A common greeting in Maa is: "Keserian ingera? Keserian ingishu?" which means: "How are the children? How are the cattle?"

Maasai also keep sheep and goats but they do not have the value of cattle.

Boys are taught at an early age to take care of the animals. Watching over the cattle is a responsibility which is not taken lightly.

The Maasai and their cattle are as much part of the Tanzanian landscape as the wild animals.

Maasai herdboy

Tanzania has more than 120 tribes, all differing in language, culture and customs. This benefits the country by balancing the power among the tribes and one result is less of the ethnic conflict that plagues much of Africa.

The shortness of this history of intervention was the making of Tanzania. The spectacular wilderness is as it was, with a few exceptions where poor management has allowed in too many tourists and commercial operators. The Tanzanians, however, recognize that wildlife is their greatest resource and have a strong commitment to preserving it. Our western image of Africa is epitomized by the enormous plains and valleys of Tanzania. Even those of us who grew up in Africa share a sense of awe about the Ngorongoro Crater and the spectacular ramparts of the Rift Valley walls defining the flat savannah plains.

The Maasai is an integral presence in this landscape, possibly the only human who belongs. Accepted by conservationists as the least destructive kind of *Homo sapiens* in the wilderness, the Maasai have nevertheless fallen foul of the authorities. They consider themselves God's chosen people and believe that the whole world was created for them. Although they have many traditions that teach honour, decency and respect, these dignified traditions do not necessarily apply in their dealings outside the tribe. When national park and conservation areas were designated, the Maasai had to answer to a new authority. As medicine improved their lifespan and decreased the infant mortality rate, their populations increased. The new control of the rinderpest simultaneously increased their livestock numbers. Where the Maasai had previously lived in harmony within conservation boundaries, their needs were growing and tensions ensued. Their ritual requirement of killing lions to

Maasai warrior

prove their manhood inevitably alienated
the National Park authorities. New controls
prevented these age-old rights of passage,
and some Maasai were forced to leave their
traditional lands. Posing for tourist dollars
is not quite in the same league as hunting
lions, but there is still enough of their old
dignity and attitude left to make them
imposing people. It is a grand sight to see a
small group of Maasai warriors, dressed in
bright red, emerging out of a distant
mirage as they silently move across the
open grasslands and despite the
encroachment of 'civilization', the Maasai
still treasure their lifestyle. Young boys take
on the responsibility of protecting their
family's herds as they wait for their turn to
become warriors. Bravery is extremely
important to a Maasai and this is

illustrated by a game the boys used to play when rhino were still plentiful. A boy would sneak up on a sleeping rhino and place a small stone on its back. The next participant had to remove it without waking the rhino. The stone was then put back, and so the game continued until the rhino finally woke up. It was a dangerous game but typical of the Maasai impulse to prove bravery. Just as the Serengeti ecosystem and the annual migration of wildebeest and zebra cross national boundaries, the Maasai cannot be restricted to one country and they move freely between Tanzania and Kenya.

Wildebeest and egrets

Arrivals and departures. Zebra and sacred ibis at the western edge of Larmakau swamp, Tarangire National Park

TARANGIRE

Larmakau swamp area (Larmakau is a corruption of the Maasai word *ol makau*, which means hippo) is an important wetland. Even in the dry season, the enormous swamp never dries and provides year-round water for the resident and migrating animals. Large flocks of sacred ibis, spoonbills and several other species inhabit the shoreline.

This swamp and the Tarangire River, which meanders southwards through the entire park, lure animals in from the dry surrounding areas. As the rainless days continue, Tarangire's populations rapidly swell. Animal concentrations during August to October can rival those of the Serengeti which makes this park one of the finest game-viewing areas in the whole of Africa.

Tarangire Tanzania. Home to Africa's most beloved giants — The elephant & the baobab tree.

Game concentrations are subject to seasonal migration. Best time — June to Oct (Dry season). During this period, Tarangire is inhabited by huge herds of zebra, wildebeest and buffalo and substantial numbers of elephant.

The dry season, however, is the worst time for the tsetse fly. These biting flies probably help keep the number of visitors down and help make this one of Africa's most unspoilt wilderness areas.

Dry season baobab trees.

Wet season baobabs look like giant broccoli.

Sacred Ibis and Zebra — Larmakau swamp

Spoonbill

Tarangire river is the only permanent water supply in the region. This scene was painted from the view at Tarangire Lodge. (Spectacular location — worst food)

At the height of the 'long rains' season starting about April, the animals disperse over a vast area, from Lake Manyara in the north-west to the Maasai Steppe in the south-east and the Badlands to the south. In June when the long rains have ended and the food supply withers and dries, the animals are once again drawn back to Tarangire in their annual cycle.

Extracts from the notes above:
Tarangire – Tanzania. Home to Africa's most beloved giants – the elephant and the baobab tree.

June to October (dry season). During this period, Tarangire is inhabited by huge herds of zebra, wildebeest and buffalo and substantial numbers of elephant. The dry season, however, is the worst time for the tsetse fly. These biting flies probably help keep the number of visitors down and help make this one of Africa's most unspoilt wilderness areas.

Wet season baobabs look like giant broccoli.

Tarangire River is the only permanent water supply in the region.

Tarangire river traffic, as viewed from the park campsite in the northern part of Tarangire

Gazelle studies

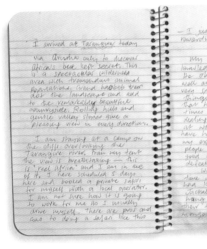

Extracts from the notebooks above and right:
I arrived at Tarangire today via Arusha only to discover Africa's best-kept secret. This is a spectacular wilderness area with tremendous animal populations. Grand baobab trees dot the landscape and add to the remarkably beautiful countryside. Rolling hills and gentle valley slopes give a pleasing view in every direction.

We spent a good deal of time with a pride of lions who had killed a young wildebeest. Jackals, hyaena and vultures hung around patiently waiting their turn.

Serval

Elephant have strong bonds and their young stay close to their mothers.

A young lion that has recently fed shows no interest in the approaching wildebeest as they make their daily trek to drink.

NGORONGORO

Ngorongoro Conservation Area is a place of such splendour that at first it seems impossible to comprehend. The approach by road from Arusha winds up a mountain side and the vegetation quickly transforms into a rain-soaked forest. Without warning you arrive at the top of the crater, where a monument to the Grzimeks looks down upon the crater floor. Lodges are placed along this stretch of road as it follows the crater rim. Most visitors get their first clear view of the crater from these strategically placed lodges. It has to be one of the grandest sights on earth, an ever-changing panorama as cloud shadows and dust devils dance across the crater floor. On my first visit we arrived too late to descend to the bottom and I can remember how impatient I was, waiting for dawn the following day. The Ngorongoro Conservation Area is a vast ecosystem and the Maasai and their livestock are part of it. The Ngorongoro Crater is a reserve within a reserve. The caldera walls are not so steep as to prevent most animals from moving into or out of the area, but the abundant food and water throughout the year means they do not have to follow the migratory habits common to the surrounding Serengeti system. Some species common to the area are, for some unknown reason, not found within the crater. These include impala, topi, and giraffe. Breeding herds of elephant are also absent probably because the cows are reluctant to take their calves down the steep walls. The Ngorongoro Crater is the most perfectly designed natural reserve neatly enclosing a circle about 11 miles (15 km) in diameter. The open grasslands of the floor and the vehicle-tolerant animals allow viewers to get close to the game. This is one of the few places I have travelled in Africa where I am able to sketch animals without using binoculars. On my first full day in the crater, I had an opportunity to work with all of the 'Big Five' except leopard. Viewing of this calibre is unusual and underscores the wonder of the area.

There is a down side, unfortunately: tourists are common too. Drivers eager to please customers by driving off the roads for better viewing have created an unacceptable situation. The fragile land needs to be protected and drivers must be controlled. To the dismay of some, camping within the crater is no longer

With its open grasslands, lion are very visible in the Ngorongoro Crater.

allowed. As ever, rules have to be implemented to protect the environment when people abuse it.

Ngorongoro is one of the few places where the black rhino can readily be seen in the wild. Threatened throughout the country, it is also in jeopardy here. National Park rangers patrol the crater floor every night, searching for poachers who target the rhino in the hope of a big pay-day. One hopes the intensive patrols will enable the rhino to persist.

Some of the bull elephants that frequent the fever tree forest have exceptionally large tusks and to see them feeding under the big acacia trees with the crater wall in the background is a real artistic treat. I cannot help but envy the early visitors to this place – what an Eden it must have been! As an artist I was in a frenzy to capture the magnificence of it all.

View of the crater floor from the Ngorongoro Lodge. K.D.

Fever trees - Lerai Forest, Ngorongoro Crater. K.D.

I felt almost as if this wonderland was made for wildlife artists. In due course I developed the ability to 'not see' other tourists in my quest to paint the crater, to claim it as my own, so to speak.

Pockets of zebra moved through the edge of the forest and took turns at using a fallen fever tree as a rubbing post. The zebra are far more colourful than their southern African cousins and their foals in particular are very beautiful with long manes which are quite orange in the sunlight.

We spent several hours with an unusual group of lions made up of four adult males, one adult lioness, and one cub that did not belong to the others. I was told that the cub was an orphan and had been semi-accepted by these males; it had already been with them for about a month. The female had no maternal desires and the cub spent his time lying close to the males. This is not normal as lions are aggressive to others that do not belong to their own pride, and strange cubs are typically killed by the

males. Even at this young age, this cub was at home amongst the tourist vehicles and at one point lay in the shade of the truck in front of us.

Another small pride of lions had made a kill in the muddy Gorigor swamp. After eating their fill before an audience of hyaena, they sauntered away looking decidedly unmajestic, all covered in mud and with enormous bellies. The hyaena were quick to get their share of the kill and the scavengers became one muddy mess. Vultures descended from out of the blue in enormous numbers but the pickings were slim on the half submerged carcass. The following morning there was no evidence of the previous day's activity and the cycle of life on the African plains went on.

The Ngorongoro Crater floor is one of the few wild places in Africa where the rare black rhino can be seen.

The social life of the lion is well documented. Cubs of various ages can be found in a large pride. They make superb subjects for an artist as they will spend as much as 3 or 4 days in one place if feeding on a large kill such as a giraffe or buffalo.

Play is an important part of a cub's life and just like domestic kittens, they are attracted to movement. Mock attacks on siblings and adults alike provide endless hours of amusement..... it is one of my favourite ways to spend an afternoon in the wild.

Lion siblings

Immature ♂ - Panthera leo.

1997 Macdonald

The Serengeti is possibly best described in two words that are the title for Hugo van Lawick's book: *Savage Paradise*. The name comes from the Maasai word *siringet*, which means 'endless plains'. The Serengeti is a massive grassland that supports an estimated three million animals, of which the majority partake in the famous migration. These herbivore populations support huge numbers of predators and these predators are easily seen in the open grasslands. I told one of my artist contemporaries of the cats I had seen during a four-day period around the Seronera area. Having never travelled to East Africa, he gave me that look one gets from someone who thinks they are being told a tall story. One eventually begins casually passing up opportunities to watch lions as they become so commonplace.

Cheetah are less numerous but they too are fairly easy to see. As in some of Kenya's more popular parks, the cheetah in the Serengeti are accustomed to viewers and not timid like those persecuted elsewhere in Africa. Leopard can be seen, but they are elusive, being more nocturnal, and do not present themselves as readily. Wild dogs, once prolific, are now greatly reduced in the Serengeti, having been decimated by an epidemic of canine distemper. Black rhino, once a common sight, have been heavily poached and as in much of the rest of Africa, they are just a

Cheetah resting

memory. I was disturbed to see how badly a herd of elephant reacted to the noise of the burners from hot air balloons. These services have no place in a designated World Heritage conservation area.

There is always room for doubt about the future of wildlife and parks in Africa. Who knows what the effects of more tourism will be, or when a game department will be afflicted with such grave financial woes as to stop functioning effectively? But there's plenty of room for hope, too. Lodges may come and go; the quality of service may wax and wane. A place that was a glorious experience in 1975 may be on the tatty side today. A place that offered prime rhino viewing in 1975 may have no rhino today, or one that had no cheetah may see increasing numbers.

Wars and political turmoil sometimes allow wildness to persist where development and agriculture might otherwise have settled over the landscape, as in Mozambique. Marginal cattle farming sometimes grows submarginal, and the land may revert to wildlife, as in the Pilanesberg National Park in South Africa. Designation as a biosphere reserve or World Heritage Site may boost a park's access to international funding. Wiser heads than mine have their work cut out for them in this dynamic mix of circumstances.

THE SERENGETI — comes from the Masai word
SIRINGET which means extensive plain, endless
expanse.
The Serengeti in Tanzania is geographically
connected to the Maasai Mara in Kenya.
These 2 national parks are known for the
massive animal wildebeest migrations.

MAASAI MARA (KENYA)

THE DRY SEASON MIGRATION
JUNE → NOVEMBER

The wildebeest migration seen today
is a recent phenomenon. There was
little evidence of such migration
until the early 1970's !!

SERENGETI
(TANZANIA)

MAASAI MARA

SERENGETI

THE WET SEASON MIGRATION
DECEMBER → MAY

NGORONGORO
CONSERVATION
AREA

Initially made well known
by Dr Bernard Grzimek and
his book "Serengeti shall not die". The Serengeti
thanks to the research and energies of Dr. Grzimek
became a national park in 1951
His son Michael followed in his footsteps only
to be killed in a plane crash at the age of 24 yrs.

*K*aribu is the Swahili word for welcome and it aptly
describes Tanzania. The local people are friendly and
helpful and those I have employed have been
enthusiastic and pleasant companions.

I hope their positive attitudes and good intentions
will help them prevail and address questions of human
population, forest clearing, poaching, tourist numbers
and dynamite fishing in the country's fragile ecosystem.

Tanzania is a special place that I will visit many more
times to capture its natural wonders in paint and to
witness the ongoing cycle of life.

*The Serengeti in Tanzania is geographically connected to the
Maasai Mara in Kenya. These two national parks are known
for the massive annual wildebeest migrations.*

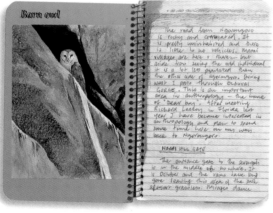
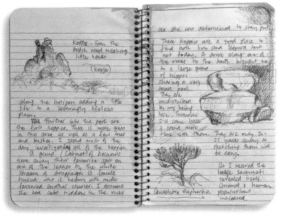

Extracts from the notebooks above:
The road from Ngorongoro is rocky and corrugated... Maasai villages are here and there but aside from seeing the odd individual it is a lot less populated than the other side of Ngorongoro.

Naabi Hill Gate. The entrance gate to the Serengeti is in the middle of nowhere. It is October and the rains have long gone, leaving this area of the park almost grassless...

I have witnessed servals jumping to catch rodents etc. But today was the first time I saw the caracal in action. The agility is remarkable and it must jump all of five feet into the air. The action is too quick to draw so I took polaroids to sketch from...

The rocky koppies in the Serengeti give the lion shade from the sun and an elevated lookout to study the plains for game.

The bateleur eagle has a characteristic mode of flight and is commonly seen gliding over the veld.

Serengeti journal

Extract from the notebook below:
The large herds of wildebeest and zebra are still in the Mara… Actually this is a good time of the year to view game as the grass is short. When the rains come … the grass grows much higher and it makes it harder to find the predators.

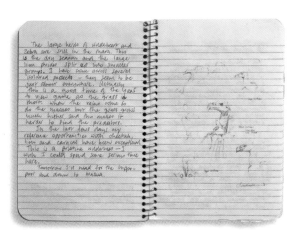

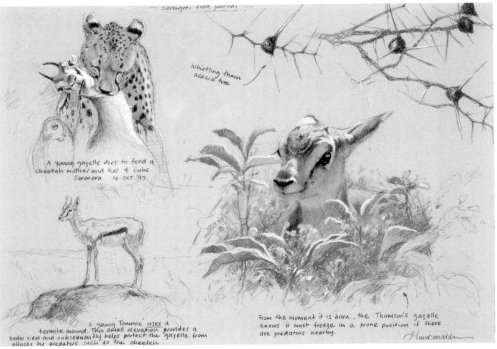

A young gazelle dies to feed a cheetah mother and her 4 cubs. Seronera 14 Oct. '97

Whistling thorn acacia tree

A young Tommie uses a termite mound. This small elevation provides a better view and subsequently helps protect the gazelle from attacks by predators such as the cheetah.

From the moment it is born, the Thomson's gazelle knows it must freeze in a prone position if there are predators nearby.

Studies of hippo (Hippopotamus amphibius)

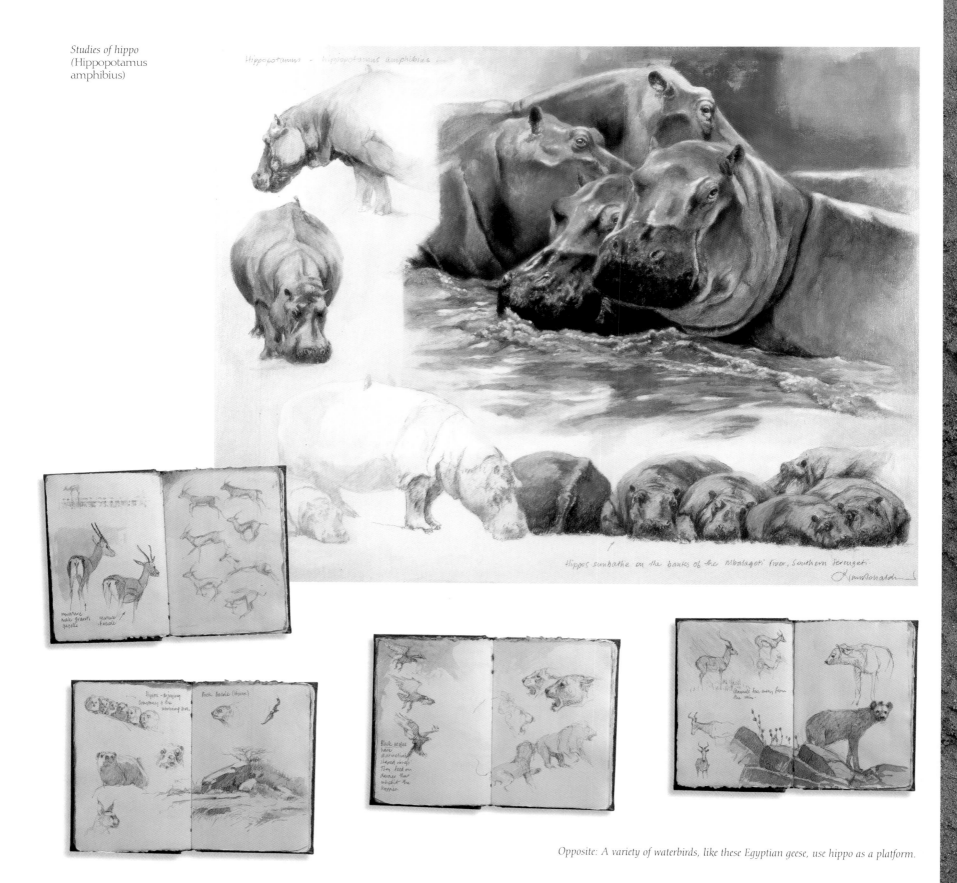

Hippopotamus - Hippopotamus amphibius

Hippos sunbathe on the banks of the Mbalageti river, Southern Serengeti.

Opposite: A variety of waterbirds, like these Egyptian geese, use hippo as a platform.

Living in harmony

Cheetah kill

CON

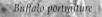

ON ART AND
SERVATION

I AM OFTEN ASKED what my favourite animal is, and my reply is generally hesitant as I need to consider this from more than one perspective.

First, as the question is normally asked in relation to my paintings, my choice is the zebra. The patterns and colouring of all the zebra subspecies have a graphic quality which is artistically desirable. Light plays a significant role in this choice as the white in the zebra is tinted by the colours of the sun and its surroundings. These subtle colour variations and the fact that zebra are synonymous with Africa make them a joy to paint. I also love the smaller creatures of the country. Suricates, the delightful mongoose of the Kalahari, are difficult to paint but an absolute joy to study. Another animal I find thoroughly absorbing but seldom capture on canvas is the chacma baboon of southern Africa and I tend to waste too much time enjoying their company.

Study of a young cheetah

econd, I would have to base an answer about favourite animals on those that give me the biggest rush when I encounter them in the wild. They are, in no particular order, elephant, lion, leopard, cheetah and buffalo. Elephant and buffalo are fairly common and easily seen. Leopard and cheetah are rare and elusive and I get tremendously excited when I see them in the wild. The lion is indeed the king of Africa's beasts and has an inherently noble manner that borders on arrogance. Lions, however, are as difficult to paint as they are to see in the wild because they are the colour of Africa. Out of all the great beasts of Africa, the lion is the most frightening and I have on more than one occasion found myself in a truly paralysing situation. People are attacked more frequently by leopard than by lion, but the lion is more likely to press the attack through to a kill. One man who did survive a mauling by a lion is my friend Willie de Beer. His story is chronicled by Capstick in *Death in the Long Grass* and today his head and face bear witness to the terrible beating he received.

This book gave me the opportunity to exercise myself artistically. Paintings and drawings range from rough field work, which I consider pure art, to finished paintings and portraits completed in the studio. In places I have been influenced by some of my favourite artists, and my subsequent work is in part an acknowledgement of my respect for them.

I am more influenced by other artists than I am by the animals in the wild. Although I paint for artistic reasons my subject is very important to me, and Africa for all its faults is close to my heart. Simply copying a photograph may prove financially rewarding for those who labour away at it faithfully, but it leaves me wanting for more. Capturing the feeling of a situation requires understanding the subject well and representing it in an original, artistic manner. There are many great realistic artists in the wildlife field, but also some whose work quickly bores me. It is difficult for many viewers to see the difference. The way I decide the worth of a painting of Africa is by the feeling it evokes – whether it makes me homesick.

The money raised by artists is a small way for us to pay back and protect the subjects from which we derive our living.

A cheetah uses available elevation to have a better view of the plains.

Everyone needs to get involved as most African countries are poor and budgets for wildlife and the environment are at the bottom of the list. In Zimbabwe, for example, my cousin Mike Fynn who was the warden at the Gonarezhou National Park had to use his own vehicle most of the time to complete his duties because the government transportation was unreliable due to the lack of funds.

I am as opinionated on conservation as I am on art. One day a person close to me who is a Republican stated that 'Conservation is a Democratic thing'. Now, much as I dislike people using conservation for personal gain, be it political or financial, I am shocked by a statement like this. We really do need to educate people about the atrocities and greedy destruction that are devastating our world at an alarming rate. This is not the problem of one political party or that of one country or continent. It should be the concern of everyone. And we cannot be sentimental about it. Conservation has

Irate jumbo bull

Blacksmith plover will stand their ground against elephant when their nesting sites are threatened.

An elephant bull is disturbed by the sandgrouse it has flushed while feeding.

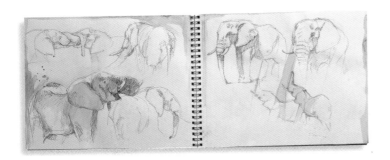

The battle for survival is portrayed in the face of an old lion.

which in turn is fed back into protecting the wildlife and the environment and provides a living for many people in Africa, people who might otherwise make their living by poaching. Furthermore, hunters are after trophy specimens which are generally older animals, past their prime, no longer necessary for reproduction and soon likely to face a violent death. Personally I derive no pleasure from shooting animals but I know many professional hunters and sportsmen, and through my association with them I have come to respect them as conservationists.

The biggest dangers facing wildlife in Africa are the increase in the human population and the corruption within governing bodies. Greed and mismanagement open the door for exploitation and the consequences are long term and in many cases permanent. Protection of the land and its inhabitants

no place for fanatics or flowery sentimentalists for they are not taken seriously and the message is lost. It is not the hunter who goes to Africa to collect trophies that is the problem. Many are quick to place blame on hunters, but these outbursts are misguided and a waste of energy. Because they are more knowledgeable and want to protect the bush and its inhabitants, hunters are often better conservationists than those who choose to fight them. The life span of most animals in the wild is extremely short and death comes in only one form – violent. The hunter who happens along is paying enormous amounts of money,

needs scientific involvement, sound managerial policies and both local and international funding. There is no question that people come first and that local residents need to benefit from these natural resources. Long-term policies therefore must incorporate the local people. Once they fully appreciate the tremendous asset they have and see the rewards in protecting it, both the people and the wildlife will be better off. It must be

understood that Africans, quite understandably, do not like being told what to do in their own land by foreigners. However, the preservation of Africa is also our concern and there are ways for us to assist without offending them. In the relatively short time that I have travelled around Africa, there have been major changes, not always for the good. I cannot show my children the Africa of my youth. For all the privileges

Eye contact

and advantages they have, I feel sorry for them as they and future generations will know a different Africa. But we cannot dwell on the past. We need to look at the present and involve ourselves in preserving the wilderness for our children and grandchildren.

Nomadic lions often pair up, increasing their chances of taking over another lion's territory and having a pride of their own.

Buffalo montage

One of Africa's more exhilarating experiences is to accidentally
walk into a group of buffalo bulls in the thick bush.

Mana Pools leopard

*T*he conservation message is important and needs to be deployed in the best possible way so that its impact is not lost. When a politician goes on and on about the ozone layer or some fanatic goes overboard on a particular concern, we become apathetic and may dismiss the subject. We cannot afford this and it is my hope that people become informed. It is not the poacher eking out a pitiful living who is our biggest concern; it is a more dangerous man – the corrupt official who is paid off by unscrupulous dealers in curios and animal products. Many rangers and wardens are men of character. However, the officials they answer to are often the ones taking financial advantage of people's heritage.

My opinions are based on observation and experience. The ability to see what is in front of you and that which is obscured is what makes an artist. As citizens of the earth, we must learn to be all-seeing and to take heed of Marjorie Rawlings's perspective in *Cross Creek*: 'It seems to me that the earth may be borrowed but not bought... It gives itself in response to love and tending ... we are tenants and not possessors.'

Are we better off for the fact that many more people want a view of Africa's wildlife today than was once the case? Unquestionably. In an era of virtual reality and electronic experience, all who take in a mincing dik-dik or a rumbling elephant, a stretching gerenuk or a sauntering giraffe with our own eyes will view the natural world differently than we did before. Africa has much to offer every kind of enthusiast, from the most casual visitor who just wants to see the 'Big Five' in two days to the most serious bird-watching guide adding hundreds of species to a 'life list'.

I count myself among the extremely fortunate to have been able to roam the places profiled here and absorb the images to overflowing.

Mister Attitude. Based on size alone, the leopard would not be included in Africa's legendary 'Big Five'. Qualification is simply a question of how dangerous an animal is to hunt.
The leopard is a loner, shying away from any human contact as it silently moves through the night. But when they are cornered or wounded, they become a worthy adversary, ferociously attacking with blinding speed and a really bad attitude.

The note above reads:
When the trunk is hanging limp the folds of the skin are vertical.

Africa   *Study for Africa*

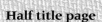

THE ARTWORKS

Half title page
PALETTE
Oil on palette
11 x 16 inches

4 *top*
VERVET MONKEY
Oil on panel
10 x 8 inches

9 *left*
MAASAI MORAN
Ink on paper
15 x 6 inches

11 *top*
ABSTRACT ELEPHANT
Mixed medium on board
10 x 8 inches

12/13
LIONS OF THE SERENGETI
Mixed medium on board
21 x 51 inches

15
QUAGGA
Oil on linen
9 x 12 inches

16
ORIGINS OF MANKIND
Mixed medium on panel
16 x 20 inches

17
QUAGGA CLONE
Oil on panel
9 x 12 inches

20/21
BURCHELL'S ZEBRA
Pastel on sandboard
13 x 18 inches

21
LION PORTRAITURE
Mixed medium on board
18 x 13 inches

22/23 *bottom*
CAPE POINT
Pastel on sandboard
10 x 30 inches

25
TSITSIKAMMA COAST
Pastel on sandboard
30 x 20 inches

26
KING CHEETAH
Pastel on sandboard
13 x 18 inches

27
ADDO ELEPHANT
Pastel on sandboard
20 x 30 inches

28
MOUNTAIN ZEBRA
Mixed medium on board
14 x 18 inches

29 *top*
CAPE MOUNTAIN ZEBRA
Pastel on sandboard
20 x 30 inches

29 *bottom*
GNU
Pastel on sandboard
12 x 24 inches

30
SERVAL
Oil on panel
12 x 9 inches

31 *bottom*
YOUNG NYALA EWE
Oil on panel
11 x 15 inches

33 *bottom left*
WARTHOG HOST
Oil on panel
12 x 16 inches

35
MKUZI ZEBRA
Mixed medium on board
20 x 30 inches

36 *bottom right*
YOUNG GIRAFFE
Pastel on sandboard
18 x 13 inches

37
TALL BLONDES
Mixed medium on panel
18 x 14 inches

38 *top*
PASSING THROUGH
Oil on panel
11 x 14 inches

38 *bottom*
OLD KRUGER BULL
Oil on panel
9 x 12 inches

39
KRUGER TUSKERS
Oil on panel
17 x 23 inches

40
WINTER LEOPARD
Mixed medium on board
20 x 30 inches

41 *top*
NOON SHADE
Pastel on sandboard
20 x 30 inches

42
LEOPARD PORTRAIT
Oil on canvas
18 x 14 inches

42/43
KRUGER LEOPARD
Mixed medium on board
20 x 30 inches

46
SABLE MONTAGE
Mixed medium on board
13 x 18 inches

47
ROAN ANTELOPE
Pastel on sandboard
13 x 18 inches

48 *top centre*
CHEETAH PORTRAITURE
Mixed medium on panel
16 x 12 inches

49 *top*
KALAHARI GEMSBUCK
Pastel on sandboard
20 x 30 inches

50
SPRINGBUCK
Pastel on sandboard
30 x 20 inches

50/51
IN FULL FLIGHT
Charcoal on panel
24 x 48 inches

52
VULTURES IN FLIGHT
Mixed medium on panel
48 x 30 inches

54 *top*
LEOPARD PORTRAITURE
Mixed medium on board
14 x 15 inches

54 *bottom*
GEMSBUCK HERD
Pen and ink
13 x 22 inches

55
ORYX JOURNAL
Pastel on sandboard
13 x 18 inches

56 *top*
RAPTOR MONTAGE
Mixed medium on panel
23 x 37 inches

56 *bottom*
KALAHARI LION
Mixed medium on board
13 x 18 inches

58 *top left*
GIRAFFE AT NXAI PAN
Pastel on paper
21 x 29 inches

58 *bottom left*
GIRAFFE DRINKING
Pen and ink
11 x 9 inches

58/59
OSTRICH
Pastel on sandboard
10 x 26 inches

60 *top*
A TRIBUTE TO BAINES
Mixed medium on panel
24 x 48 inches

60/61
ZEBRA AND DUST
Pastel on sandboard
14 x 40 inches

62
GRUMPY OLD MEN
Mixed medium on board
13 x 18 inches

63 *top*
DELTA ELEPHANT
Pastel on sandboard
20 x 30 inches

64 *top*
WILD DOG
Oil on panel
18 x 24 inches

65
MOREMI TWILIGHT
Pastel on sandboard
20 x 30 inches

66
LECHWE
Mixed medium on board
20 x 30 inches

67
DELTA BUFFALO
Mixed medium on board
30 x 20 inches

69
BOTSWANA JUMBO
Mixed medium on board
13 x 18 inches

71
WATERBUCK MONTAGE
Mixed medium on board
13 x 18 inches

72
KING OF THE BEASTS
Oil on panel
7 x 12 inches

72/73
LIONESS
Mixed mediun on board
13 x 18 inches

75
SAVUTI VLEI
Pastel on sandboard
20 x 30 inches

76
PORTRAIT OF A KING
Mixed medium on board
12 x 12 inches

77
KING OF SAVUTI
Mixed medium on board
30 x 40 inches

78
STUDY FOR *IN YOUR FACE*
Mixed medium on board
13 x 18 inches

79
NOGATSAA ELEPHANT
Pastel on sandboard
20 x 30 inches

80 *top left*
BOTSWANA BAOBABS
Pen and ink
11 x 14 inches

80 *top right*
BUFFALO SKULL
Oil on canvas
12 x 16 inches

80 *bottom left*
WARTHOG MONTAGE
Mixed medium on board
13 x 18 inches

81 *top*
SERONDELLA JUMBO
Pastel on sandboard
20 x 30 inches

82
BUFFALO HERD
Charcoal on board
30 x 42 inches

83
CHOBE DAWN
Pastel on sandboard
20 x 30 inches

84 *top*
GOSHAWK
Pencil on paper
10 x10 inches

84 *bottom*
LIONS OF NAMIBIA
Mixed medium on panel
20 x 16 inches

84/85
KUDU MONTAGE
Mixed medium on board
13 x 18 inches

87
NAMIBIAN TWILIGHT
Pastel on sandboard
20 x 30 inches

88
WILDEBEEST
Charcoal and wash
13 x 19 inches

89 *bottom right*
SAVANNAH PRINCE
Mixed medium on board
18 x 13 inches

90/91
CHEETAH PATROL
Pastel on board
30 x 55 inches

92 *top*
ETOSHA MONTAGE
Mixed medium on board
13 x 18 inches

92 *bottom right*
BAT-EARED FOXES
Pastel on sandboard
10 x 19 inches

93 *right*
SPRINGBUCK MONTAGE
Mixed medium on board
18 x 13 inches

94
DRY SEASON DUST DEVILS
Pastel on sandboard
20 x 30 inches

95 *top*
GEMSBUCK
Oil on panel
18 x 12 inches

95 *bottom right*
ROYAL POSE
Acrylic on panel
14 x 11 inches

96/97
TALKING BACK
Mixed medium on board
13 x 36 inches

98/99
ETOSHA PAN
Mixed medium on board
15 x 54 inches

98 *bottom right*
KUDU PORTRAITURE
Oil on canvas
16 x 12 inches

100/101
OKONDEKA OSTRICH
Pastel on board
12 x 43 inches

100 *bottom left*
ETOSHA FIELD PAINTING
Oil on canvas
13 x 30 inches

101 *bottom right*
IMPALA IN FLIGHT
Pencil on paper
6 x 15 inches

102 *bottom*
ETOSHA PAN ZEBRA
Pastel on sandboard
20 x 30 inches

102/103
WATERHOLE TRAFFIC
Pastel on board
30 x 55 inches

105
FLAMINGOES
Pastel on paper
30 x 42 inches

108 *top right*
LIZARD BUZZARD
Oil on board
12 x 8 inches

108 *bottom*
FIELD JOURNAL
Mixed medium on board
13 x18 inches

110/111
ZIMBABWE MONTAGE
Mixed medium on panel
18 x 24 inches

111
RAPTOR MONTAGE
Oil on panel
17 x 23 inches

113 *top*
RHINO MONTAGE
Mixed medium on panel
13 x 18 inches

113 *bottom*
HYRAX MONTAGE
Mixed medium on panel
13 x 18 inches

114 *left*
ZIMBABWE MONTAGE 2
Mixed medium on map
33 x 24 inches

114 *bottom right*
OLD JUMBO COW
Oil on canvas
8 x 10 inches

115
HWANGE SABLE
Mixed medium on panel
20 x 30 inches

116 *right*
EAGLE OWL
Pencil on paper
12 x 8 inches

116 *bottom left*
SABLE PORTRAITURE
Pastel on board
13 x 18 inches

117
HWANGE ZEBRA
Pastel on sandboard
20 x 30 inches

118
LEOPARD STUDIES
Oil on panel
23 x 17 inches

119 *top*
HWANGE TUSKER
Pastel on board
20 x 30 inches

119 *bottom left*
TEST OF STRENGTH
Acrylic on board
19 x 34 inches

120
VICTORIA FALLS
Pastel on sandboard
20 x 30 inches

121
TRIBAL DANCER
Pastel on paper
14 x 21 inches

122
ELEPHANT UTOPIA
Pastel on paper
29 x 42 inches

123 *left*
BUFFALO MONTAGE
Oil on panel
11 x 14 inches

124/125
SPURWING BUFFALO
Pastel on board
13 x 36 inches

126
KARIBA SPOONBILLS
Pastel on board
20 x 30x inches

127
SUNSET OVER KARIBA
Pastel on sandboard
20 x 30 inches

128 *right*
RHINO STUDIES
Pencil on paper
10 x12 inches

129 *top*
ZEBRA AND MAHOGANY
Mixed medium on panel
20 x 30 inches

129 *bottom*
YOUNG ZEBRA
Mixed medium on panel
13 x 18 inches

130 *bottom right*
BAOBAB TREE
Watercolour on paper
12 x 11 inches

131
LONG POOL
Mixed medium on panel
20 x 30 inches

133 *top*
SUMMER SIESTA
Mixed medium on board
20 x 30 inches

133 *bottom*
SERVAL WITH GILDING
Oil on panel
16 x 12 inches

134/135
ZAMBEZI CROSSING
Mixed medium on board
20 x 51 inches

135 *bottom*
RIVER CROSSING
Pencil on paper
18 x 21 inches

136
BUFFALO BULLS
Oil on panel
14 x 24 inches

137
OLD MANA LION
Oil on panel
12 x 16 inches

138
NUANETSI RIVER
Mixed medium on board
20 x 30 inches

139 *bottom*
JUMBO BULL STUDY
Mixed medium on board
10 x 14 inches

140
BUFFALO WATER WALK
Mixed medium on board
20 x 30 inches

142 *left*
LION CUBS STUDY
Acrylic on panel
19 x 24 inches

142 *right*
ZEBRA AND STARLINGS
Oil on panel
14 x 11 inches

143 *bottom right*
BARN OWL STUDY
Oil on board
12 x 9 inches

144 *top left*
NFD MONTAGE
Mixed medium on panel
15 x 19 inches

144 *right*
SAMBURU MAIDENS
Pencil on paper
12 x 12 inches

145 *top right*
SAMBURU LANDSCAPE
Watercolour on paper
7 x 12 inches

145 *left*
VULTURINE GUINEA FOWL
Oil on panel
16 x 10 inches

146 *left*
SAMBURU YOUTH
Charcoal/oil on panel
32 x 19 inches

147
SAMBURU WARRIORS
Oil on panel
20 x 16 inches

148 *left and centre*
SAMBURU STUDIES 1
Coloured pencil
15 x 9 / 15 x 9 inches

148 *right and* **149**
SAMBURU STUDIES 2
Coloured pencil
15 x 9 / 15 x 9 inches

151
SHADOWS OVER SAMBURU
Pastel on board
20 x 30 inches

152
LEOPARD STALKING
Mixed medium on board
20 x 30 inches

153 *bottom left*
GIRAFFE MONTAGE
Mixed medium on board
13 x 18 inches

154/155
GREVY'S ZEBRA
Mixed medium on board
20 x 51 inches

156/157
WAITING OUT THE STORM
Mixed medium on board
15 x 60 inches

157 *bottom right*
MUDDY MORSEL
Mixed medium on panel
12 x 16 inches

158 *top*
CHEETAH STUDY
Mixed medium on board
13 x 18 inches

158 *bottom*
LION STUDY
Pencil on paper
10 x 8 inches

159
NEW ARRIVALS
Pastel on sandboard
30 x 40 inches

160/161
CHEETAH COUNTRY
Mixed medium on board
30 x 55 inches

161
CHEETAH IN FULL FLIGHT
Pencil on paper
Collection

162 *top left*
ZEBRA FIGHTING
Mixed medium on board
13 x 18 inches

162 *bottom left*
OLD MAASAI WOMAN
Mixed medium on panel
9 x12 inches

163 *left*
ZEBRA FIGHTING 2
Acrylic on canvas
12 x 17 inches

163 *right*
ELEPHANT AND FEVER TREE
Mixed medium on board
30 x 20 inches

164
BLACK RHINO STUDY
Oil on canvas
8 x 13 inches

165 *top*
KILIMANJARO FOOTHILLS
Mixed medium on board
20 x 30 inches

165 *bottom*
LION STUDY
Acrylic on panel
10 x 8 inches

166
ZEBRA MOTHER AND FOAL
Mixed medium on board
13 x 18 inches

199 *top*
EYE CONTACT
Oil on panel
9 x 12 inches

199 *bottom*
ROYAL NOMADS
Oil on canvas
34 x 70 inches

200/201
BUFFALO TERRITORY
Oil on canvas
36 x 60 inches

201 *top right*
BUFFALO MONTAGE
Acrylic on panel
20 x 16 inches

202 *top left*
LEOPARD STUDY
Pencil on paper
8 x 8 inches

202 *bottom*
MANA POOLS LEOPARD
Mixed medium on board
18 x 13 inches

202/203
MISTER ATTITUDE
Mixed medium on board
30 x 55 inches

204/205
AFRICA
Oil on canvas
40 x 70 inches

205 *bottom right*
STUDY FOR *AFRICA*
Oil on panel
18 x 24 inches

212
THE BIG COUNTRY
Mixed medium on board
30 x 40 inches

214 *bottom*
LION WITH BUFFALO
Mixed medium on paper
6 x 12 inches

216 *top*
CLASSIC POSE
Pastel on board
20 x 30 inches

216 *bottom*
STUDY OF OLD LION
Watercolour on paper
9 x 16 inches

218/219
ZEBRA COUNTRY
Pastel on sandboard
20 x 30 inches

Elephant need a big country
to get enough food to feed
their enormous appetites.

ROLL OF HONOUR

Dedication to the living and the dead who have influenced my life.

A. O. B. Elias   *Father-in-law*

Nicole, Matthew and Mark   *My children*

Thomas Baines   *Artist and explorer*

W. J. Burchell   *Botanist, artist and explorer*

W. C. Oswell   *Gentleman hunter*

J. Stevenson-Hamilton   *Pioneer game warden*

Rupert Fothergill   *Leader of Operation Noah*

Hilary Forsyth   *Artist and friend*

Chris McBride   *Son of Africa*

Edmund Caldwell   *Pioneer of wildlife art*

Joy Adamson   *Author*

George Adamson   *Lover of lions*

Bernhard Grzimek   *Pioneer zoologist*

Wally Ferreira   *Uncle and artist*

Ted Davidson   *Pioneer game warden*

Clem Coetzee   *Protector of the animals*

Kerry Fynn   *Cousin and man of the bush*

Jock Forsyth   *Art teacher*

Harry Manners   *Hunter and author*

Paul Bosman   *Artist and friend*

Bill McGill   *Artist and unique character*

Dino Paravano   *Artist and friend*

Karen Blixen   *Author*

Louis and Mary Leakey   *Ornithologists*

Peter Beard   *Author, photographer and diarist*

Sir Percy Fitzpatrick   *Author*

Herman Charles Bosman   *Writer with deep human understanding*

Coney Flemming   *Headmaster extraordinaire*

Laurie Marker   *Friend to all cheetahs*

AN AFRICAN EXPERIENCE

AMONG THE ELEPHANTS

KAMBAKU!
KIM DONALDSON

213

BIBLIOGRAPHY

George Adamson, *My Pride and Joy, An Autobiography*, Simon & Schuster, New York, 1987

Joy Adamson, *The Peoples of Kenya*, Harcourt, Brace & World, Inc. New York

Peter Apps, *Wild Ways*, Southern Book Publishers (Pty) Ltd, Halfway House, 1992

William Charles Baldwin, *African Hunting*, Books of Zimbabwe, 1981 reprint edition

Daryl and Sharna Balfour, *African Elephants, A Celebration of Majesty*, Struik Publishers, Cape Town

Daryl and Sharna Balfour, *Chobe ~ Africa's Untamed Wilderness*, Abbeville Press, New York, 1998

Anthony Bannister and René Gordon, *The National Parks of South Africa*, Struik Publishers, Cape Town

Peter Beard, *End of the Game*, Chronicle Books, San Francisco, 1963

Paul Bosman and Anthony Hall-Martin, *Elephants of Africa*, Woodbine Publishing, 1989

Bartle Bull, *Safari, A Chronical of Adventure*, Penguin Books, 1992

Ted Davison, *Wankie: The Story of a Great Game Reserve*, Thorntree Press, Zimbabwe, 1996

Isak Dinesen, *Isak Dinesen's Africa*, Sierra Club Books, San Francisco

Lion with buffalo

Jean Dorst and Pierre Dandelot, *A Field Guide to Larger Mammals of Africa*, Houghton Mifflin Company, Boston, 1970

Alan Elliott, *The Presidential Elephants of Zimbabwe*, The Corporate Brochure Company, London, 1991

Bernhard and Michael Grzimek, *Serengeti Shall Not Die*, E. P. Dutton & Co. Inc., New York, 1961

Donald & Lenora Johnson and Blake Edgar, *Ancestors*, Villard Books, New York, 1994

David Keith Jones, *Faces of Kenya*, Hamish Hamilton Ltd, London, 1977

Dereck and Beverly Joubert, *Hunting with the Moon: The Lions of Savuti*, The National Geographic Society, 1997

Jonathan Kingdon, *Field Guide to African Mammals*, Academic Press Ltd, London, 1997

The collected works of Rudyard Kipling.

A classic pose is adopted by the elephant as it faces an intruder.

Study of old lion

Richard Leakey, *The Origin of Humankind*, Bask Books, New York, 1994

Astley Maberly, *Animals of Rhodesia*, Howard Timmins, Cape Town,1959

Thomasin Magor, *African Warriors*, Harry N. Abrams, Inc., New York, 1994

G. R. McLachlan and R. Liversidge, *Roberts Birds of South Africa*, C.N.A, South Africa, revised edition – Fifth impression 1965

John McNutt and Lesley Boggs, *Running Wild*, Southern Book Publishers (Pty) Ltd, South Africa, 1996

Credo Mutwa, *Isilwane, 'The Animal'*, Struik Publishers, Cape Town, 1996

Arthur H. Neumann, *Elephant Hunting in East Equatorial Africa*, Books of Zimbabwe, 1982 reprint edition

Mark and Delia Owens, *Cry of the Kalahari*, Fontana/Collins, UK,1985

David Paynter and Wilf Nussey, *Kruger: Portrait of a National Park*, Macmillan South Africa (Pty) Ltd, 1986

A Reader, *The Africans*, Praeger Publishers, New York, 1986

Veronica Roodt, *Trees and Shrubs of the Okavango Delta*, Shell Oil Botswana (Pty) Ltd, Gaborone, Botswana, 1998

Kermit Roosevelt, *A Sentimental Safari*, Alfred A. Knopf, Inc. 1963

Theodore Roosevelt, *The Hunting and Exploring Adventures of Theodore Roosevelt*, The Dial Press, New York, 1955

Lynn Sher, *Tall Blondes*, Andrews McMeel Publishing, Kansas City, 1997

Chris and Tilde Stuart, *Field Guide: Mammals of Southern Africa*, Struik Publishers, Cape Town, 1988

Chris and Tilde Stuart, *Africa's Vanishing Wildlife*, Southern Book Publishers (Pty) Ltd, Halfway House, 1996

Chris and Tilde Stuart, *Africa's Great Wild Places*, Southern Book Publishers, South Africa, 1998

Clive Walker, *Signs of the Wild*, Struik Publishers, Cape Town, 1981

Nick Walker, *The Painted Hills*, Mambo Press, Gweru, 1996

J. P. R. Wallis, *Thomas Baines*, Books of Zimbabwe, 1982 re-print edition

PHOTOGRAPH ACKNOWLEDGEMENTS
I am grateful to the National Archives of Zimbabwe for their permission to reproduce photographs from their collection.

Noon is a somewhat uneventful time.
Predators are resting during the heat of the
day and all activity comes to a standstill.